The American Left in the Twentieth Century

The American Left in the Twentieth Century

John P. Diggins
University of California, Irvine

Under the General Editorship of
John Morton Blum, Yale University

 HARCOURT BRACE JOVANOVICH, INC.

New York   Chicago   San Francisco   Atlanta

Frontispiece: Magnum Photos, Inc.

Preface

The American Left in the twentieth century was born in America. Contrary to popular belief, it was not the product of foreign powers and alien ideologies. Although each Left generation would have its rendezvous with European Marxism, Marxist ideas were usually embraced to support a radical movement that had already come into being. Most Left intellectuals and activists in America read Jefferson and Whitman before they read Marx or, later, Mao, and many caught the flame of William Jennings Bryan or John Fitzgerald Kennedy before they felt the fascination of Lenin or Castro. Sprouting from native soil, the Left often erupted in a fury of radical innocence and wounded idealism so peculiar to American intellectual history. We need only listen to the opening dialogue in the first major confrontation of the New Left. At the height of the Berkeley Free Speech Movement in 1964, student leader Mario Savio denounced the university "system" as a technological grotesquerie: "It becomes odious so we must put our bodies against the gears, against the wheels and machines, and make the machine stop until we're free." The image of man throwing his body against the mechanistic institution has always touched a rebellious impulse deeply rooted in the American mind and character. In the nineteenth century Emerson cursed the "corpse-cold" nature of institutions and protested a society in which "man is thus metamorphosed into a thing"; Whitman called upon young Americans to "sing" of themselves and to "resist much, obey little"; and Thoreau formulated his classic doctrine of civil disobedience in the metaphors of human resurrection and mechanistic doom: "Let your life be a counter friction to stop the machine." Karl Marx told us a great deal about the nature of society against which man rebels; Emerson's "The American Scholar" may tell us even more about the emotional and intellectual sources of alienation and idealism that have characterized the twentieth-century American Left.

The American Left has generally been approached as either a footnote to the history of the American labor movement, as an aspect of the socialist and communist experiences in the United States, or as an episode in the rich chronicle of American literary radicalism. To integrate these dimensions in an interpretive synthesis, I have drawn upon the excellent studies of Daniel Bell, Theodore Draper, and Daniel Aaron. My own focus is primarily intellectual history as expressed through generational experience. By intellectual history I do not mean the disembodied "history of ideas." Rather, the concern here is with the mind and moral temper of a generation as it arises from concrete historical experience.

Within the limitations of this slender volume, I have three aims: to describe the sensibilities and styles of thought that a radical intellectual movement assumes as a means of mobilizing its emotional energies; to explain the philosophical posture it adopts as a means of negating the prevailing "truths" that sustain the existing order; and to analyze briefly the historical factors that account for the "deradicalization" of the Left as a generational phenomenon. The main focus therefore will be not on the Left in general but on three different American Lefts: the Lyrical Left of the World War I era, the Old Left of the 1930's, and the New Left of the 1960's. The Lyrical Left had its emotional and intellectual roots in the joyous, rhapsodic milieu of New York's Greenwich Village. In contrast, the Old Left's desperate hopes and anxieties derived from the Depression and the rise of European totalitarianism; and the impulses of the New Left arose out of a deep sense of personal alienation in a society of affluence and of political frustration produced by a cold war abroad and a racial crisis at home. Each of these groups on the left had different social origins and evolved from different historical contexts; and each projected different self-images, political objectives, ideologies, and life styles. Lacking historical continuity, each Left is best approached as a unique generational rebellion, for each tended to deny paternity to its predecessor and enduring legacy to its successor. Revolutions may devour their children; in the rites of political passage that characterize generational revolts it is the children who slay their fathers.

The American Left resists precise definition, but there are ways of approaching a historical understanding of its role in past and present society. Part One of *The American Left in the Twentieth Century,* devoted mainly to theoretical and problematic issues, attempts to explain why simple definitions sacrifice nuance for neatness, why the Left may be interpreted as an intellectual and cultural phenomenon, and why the American Left found itself without a real, substantial proletariat. Part Two deals specifically with the three American Lefts of the twentieth century. Their respective histories hardly represent a success story. But in America, the land that has denied each Left a second life, we can learn from failure. Even while the Left draws its "poetry" from the perfect future, it cannot ignore the imperfect past. Marx stated the lesson well in the preface to *Capital:* "We suffer not only from the living but from the dead. *Le mort saisit le vif!"*

I should like to express my appreciation to Anne Rogers and Peter Clecak for their helpful criticisms of the manuscript; to Judy Aspinwall, Phil Ressner, and Tom Williamson for their editorial suggestions; to Susan Haggerty for digging up many priceless illustrations; to Daniel Aaron for permitting me to examine his collection of unpublished materials; and to John Morton Blum for his advice and encouragement. I am also grateful to my "Left" colleagues at the University of California, Irvine, for listening to a skeptic; and to my wife, Jacy, for listening to an academic. The book is dedicated to my son and daughter, Sean and Nicole, in the hope that their generation will prove the old man wrong.

JOHN P. DIGGINS

For Sean and Nicole

Contents

Preface   v

PART ONE   THEORY   1

1   The Problem of Definition   3

Popular Characteristics of the Left   3

Advocacy of Change   3
Political Ideals   5
Advocacy of Economic Democracy   9
Tradition of Dissent   10
Rationalism and Ideology   12

Historical Roles   14

The Left as Opposition   15
The Left as Negation   16
The Left as a Generational Experience   17
The Left as an Ally of the Working Class   20
Notes   25

2   The New Intellectuals   27

The Left Intellectual   28

Conflict with Marxian Socialists   28
Walling, Lippmann, and Eastman   31

ix

The Historical Consciousness of the Left   34

    The Role of Dewey and James   34
    The Task of Mind   36
    Notes   38

3 Strangers in the Land: The Proletariat and
    Marxism   39

    Farmers and Industrial Workers   40

    The Utopian Tradition   49

    The Marxist Background   54

    Three Leaders in American Socialism   63

        Debs   63
        DeLeon   65
        Haywood   67
        Notes   69

PART TWO   HISTORY   71

4 The Lyrical Left   73

    Early Raptures   74

        Politics and Art   75
        Diversity of Appeal   78
        The New Review and *The New Masses*   79

    Challenges and Conflict   81

        War and the State   81
        Bolshevism: The Triumph   88
        Bolshevism: The Disenchantment   94

The Odysseys of Reed and Eastman: Two Patterns of
Disillusionment   96

    Reed   96
    Eastman   100
    Notes   105

5   **The Old Left**   107

    The Depression and Communism   108

    The Popular Front   121

    The Critique of Marxism: Legacy of the Old Left   136

        Sociology: From Marx to Tocqueville   136
        Economics: From Marx to Keynes   138
        Political Science: From Marx to Madison   140
        Theology: From Marx to Kierkegaard   142
        Literature: From Marx to Melville   143
        American History: From Marx to Locke   145
        Philosophy: From Marx to James   148

    Pessimism and Relevance: The Gulf Between   151

    Notes   152

6   **The New Left**   155

    From Alienation to Activism   157

        Antecedent Lefts: Differences and Similarities   162

    From Port Huron to Peking   168

        The Civil Rights Movement   168
        Students for a Democratic Society   169

Progressive Labor Party 171
Offshoots of the Old 172
Black Militants 173

Decline with Influence 176

The Agency of Change 176
The Vietnam War 177
Repression 180
Factionalism and Suicidal Extremism 182

The "New Consciousness" and Herbert Marcuse 186

Notes 195
Photo Credits 197
Index 199

part one
THEORY

The Problem 1
of Definition

He belonged to the left, which, as they say
in Spain, is the side of the heart, as the right
is that of the liver.

George Santayana, 1920

The true Left is that which continues faithfully to invoke, not liberty or equality, but
fraternity—in other words, love.

Raymond Aron, 1957

The first obstacle in a study of the American Left in the twentieth
century is the difficulty of discovering precisely what the American
Left is. One of the most elusive of all political categories, the Left does
not lend itself to tidy, fixed definitions. The following discussion
attempts to illustrate some of the fallacies and limitations contained
in common notions about the Left.

POPULAR CHARACTERISTICS OF THE LEFT

Advocacy of Change

In the simplest terms "the Left" has generally designated those who
wish to change an existing order, and "the Right," those who wish to

preserve it. This formulation does not tell us very much. For what is at issue is not the demand for change but the motive for change. Indeed, when viewed in historical perspective, the Left may be seen less as an agent of change than as a response to it. More often than not the social and political changes demanded by the Left were primarily reactions to vast, disruptive economic and technological changes wrought by the Right. Capitalists on the Right may not have created their own "grave-diggers" when they produced an industrial working class, as Marx prophesied, but in drastically transforming the character of modern society, capitalists did more than anyone else to give birth to the Left. Nineteenth-century industrialization in particular brought not only soot and squalor but human atomization, depersonalization, and exploitation, reducing society to what Emile Durkheim called "a dust of individuals." In the United States in the late nineteenth century it was the men of the Left, the utopian and Christian socialists, who protested the rapid economic changes that were destroying the intimate bonds of human community. Significantly, one finds in the twentieth-century American Left a curious ambiguity on the question of change; one is

1 Family dinner at a nineteenth-century commune, the Oneida Community, New York.

2 Scene in a west-coast commune of the 1970's.

never sure whether it desires to transform society in order to realize new values or in order to restore lost ideals. By mid-century this ambivalence seemed to have been resolved in favor of the values of the past. At times the New Left of the 1960's, with its pastoral idyll of small, self-sufficient communities pursuing simple crafts, appeared to have turned its back on change and modernity.

Political Ideals

Since a political phenomenon may be defined in light of its ideals, it may be useful to consider whether the American Left possessed an exclusive and coherent set of political ideals. The political principles generally associated with the historic European Left are: liberty, justice, equality, and democracy. Liberty, as one of the great ideals of the French Revolution, developed in response to the classic antagonism between the aristocracy and bourgeoisie, a postfeudal stage of historical conflict that was not part of colonial America's political experience. Americans were "born free," as Tocqueville observed, and did not have to struggle for the political liberties that Europeans achieved only after years of revolutionary turmoil. Moreover, the Anglo-Saxon idea of liberty was essentially "negative liberty"—constitutional freedoms designed not to enable man to realize his "higher nature" or "true self," but to protect him *against* encroachments by the state.[1] The Left sometimes resorts

5

VOL. 1   SAN FRANCISCO, JULY 1, 1916   No. 15

YOU AND I CANNOT LIVE IN THE SAME LAND

3   The Left defends the liberal cause of a free press during the repressions of the First World War.

to constitutional rights like free speech, as did the Lyrical Left when it was harassed by the government during the First World War, or it may repudiate these "bourgeois" liberties as a form of "repressive tolerance," as did some elements of the New Left.[2] Love of liberty has been an occasional affair of the Left, not a marriage.

It is also difficult to make justice and equality ideals peculiar to the Left. For when we try to define these concepts we find that they are as elusive to the Left as they have always been to the political philosopher. If justice is understood as a legal principle, as fair and equitable treatment, conservative lawyers and jurists may have as much claim to it as does the Left. If justice is understood as a social ideal, as sympathy for the poor and oppressed, the Left can hardly deny that many twentieth-century liberal reformers and humanitarians have had a commitment to social justice—and one that appeared more capable of enduring setbacks and defeats. Equality is also a perplexing issue. It was Thomas Jefferson, not Karl Marx, who announced that "all men are created equal," and the meaning of that ringing statement has troubled intellectual historians ever since. When equality is cast as an economic proposition—as equality of opportunity—it suggests an ethos of competition, achievement, and merit that the twentieth-century Left rejected when it turned its back on liberal capitalism. On the other hand, equality invoked as a moral injunction, according to which it becomes man's "duty" to treat his fellow man as equal while raising him from his unequal station, was taken by some sensitive radical intellectuals to be patronizing.

> Duty, like sacrifice and service, always implies a personal relation of individuals. You are always doing your duty to somebody or something. Always the taint of inequality comes in. You are morally superior to the person who has duty done to him. If that duty is not filled with good-will and desire, it is morally hateful, or at very best, a necessary evil,—one of those compromises with the world which must be made in order to get through it all. But duty without good-will is a compromise with our present state of inequality, and to raise duty to the level of a virtue is to consecrate that state of inequality forevermore.[3]

Democracy, another ideal of the historic European Left, is even more difficult to use in reference to the twentieth-century American Left. In nineteenth-century Europe the Left fought alongside the working class to gain the ballot and win political power from the bourgeoisie. These goals had largely been realized in America long before the appearance of the first modern Left. Moreover, the peculiar sequence of American political and economic history has worked to frustrate the American Left. In many parts of continental Europe, where democracy lagged behind industrialization, or where, as in southern and eastern Europe, it failed to penetrate conditions of economic backwardness, workers became class conscious before they became politically conscious. In America, however, mass democracy developed at the same time as bourgeois capitalism. The "specter" of a democratic class war against capitalism and property that haunted European conservatives turned out to be more shadow than substance in America.

Early in the nineteenth century the conservative Federalist and Whig parties did fear unlimited suffrage as a threat to property rights. Then, in the tumultuous "cider campaign" of 1840, the Whigs, finally realizing there were no class-conscious "mobs" in America, nominated the popular military hero General William Henry Harrison for president. Stooping to conquer, wealthy New England Whigs sent Harrison around the country in a large wagon with a log cabin on top and a barrel of hard cider on tap for the crowds of workmen. The Whigs won the popular vote from the Jacksonians, and democracy was safely domesticated.

The People's Line--Take care of the Locomotive

4 Cartoon comment on conservative Whig cultivation of the working class in the presidential campaign of 1840. William Henry Harrison is the locomotive.

Thus, in contrast to Europe, where the struggle for democracy often accompanied the struggle for socialism, democracy in America never posed a direct threat to capitalism, since many Americans owned some property, and even those who did not could dream of doing so. The one exception to this is the South, where recent demands for the ballot by disenfranchised blacks represent a struggle to alter both class and political structures. But this exception also illustrates the dilemma of using democracy as a defining goal of the Left. In the late nineteenth century, American radicals could look upon the struggles of the working class as a genuine democratic expression because workers appeared to constitute a growing majority of the population. The New Left, however, became involved with the civil rights and social goals of powerless minorities. If the historic European Left, as David Caute argues, is to be defined as the attempt to realize "popular sovereignty," the New Left in America will have to be defined as the attempt to realize the sovereignty of the unpopular.[4]

Advocacy of Economic Democracy

Although nineteenth-century American history deprived the twentieth-century American Left of political democracy as a goal, the ideal of economic democracy was still far from realization. Liberalism may have succeeded in democratizing political institutions and expanding suffrage, but the Left realized that the masses would remain without effective power as long as man's work, wages, and welfare were controlled by those who owned the means of production. To extend democracy from the political to the economic sphere became, therefore, the characteristic goal of the Left. Whether economic democracy is automatically realized when private enterprise is socialized remains a speculative proposition. Nevertheless, in the past the American Left has assumed that true freedom begins only when capitalism ends. Hence the Left was nothing if not anticapitalist. All the Lefts of the twentieth century were influenced by socialism; all advocated various programs calling for public ownership of the means of production and democratic control of economic activity. However the new social order was envisioned, competitive individualism would be replaced by some version of the cooperative ideal in which man, freed from the economic neces-

9

sity of engaging in coerced labor, would realize his full nature in creative work. Using anticapitalism as an exclusive categorical definition of the Left, however, creates some difficulties. In America liberal reformers also have advocated public control of private enterprise, and, indeed, some of the sharpest critics of capitalism have been men of the Right. The attacks on the inhumanity of the "free" economy by slavery apologists like John C. Calhoun and George Fitzhugh, the penetrating critiques of industrial capitalism by conservative writers like Allen Tate and Irving Babbitt, and the diatribes against Wall Street by proto-fascists like Ezra Pound and Lawrence Dennis are as caustic as any editorial in *Pravda* or the *Daily Worker*. Anticapitalism has more than one meaning; it is not necessarily synonymous with the Left.

Tradition of Dissent

The American Left may lay claim to a long and rich tradition of radical dissent.[5] The challenge of individual conscience against authority and majority rule began with the Puritan antinomians of the seventeenth century; it was carried forward by the abolitionists of the nineteenth century; and it found its most recent expression in the activities of civil-rights workers and draft resisters of the 1960's. Yet dissent itself cannot serve to define the Left in any meaningful sense. Dissent is not a social philosophy but a tactic, a method of protesting and communicating to the public in order to bring law more into congruence with some ideal or higher law. Nor is dissent compatible with democracy, for dissent involves conflict between autonomous individual morality and political allegiance. As is liberty, dissent is basically negative, an assertion of the integrity of the individual's private conscience against both the coercion of the state and the "tyranny of the majority." Moreover, the dissent tradition is highly individualistic, occasionally anarchistic, and at times even spiritual and mystical, whereas the Left comes alive in collective action and seeks material solutions to social problems. The Left may hail Thoreau as the most noble dissenter of all, the heroic "majority of one," who went to jail rather than support a war and who dropped out of society rather than conform to it, but the philosopher-poet of Walden Pond deliberately refused to offer any radical program for transforming

10

5 and 6   Police harass abolitionists in late-nineteenth-century Boston *(above)* and civil-rights marchers in Selma, Alabama, in 1965 *(below)*.

7   Henry David Thoreau, nineteenth-century dissenter whose radical ideas could never be assimilated by the Marxist Left.

society other than advising men of "quiet desperation" to "simplify" their needs.[6] The twentieth-century American Left could find moral inspiration in the dissent tradition; it had to look elsewhere for political direction.

Rationalism and Ideology

Is it possible to define the Left by its belief systems and mental habits? Does the Left possess a common world view and a common theory of knowledge? Is there, in short, a systematic "mind" of the Left? It is a widespread notion that the Left stands for rationality and intelligence and has an optimistic belief in the essential goodness of human nature. On the other side, the Right is said to stand for the primacy of emotion over reason, the elemental sinfulness of man, and hence the imperfections of the "human condition." This dichotomy may have been somewhat true during the Revolutionary era, when men of the Enlightenment like Tom Paine proclaimed the infinite capacities of human intelligence, and conservatives like John Adams tried to demonstrate the infinite illusions of reason. But in the nineteenth century radical reform movements were often inspired by religious "awakenings," philosophical idealism, or the romantic cult of moral intuition; and the first Left in the twentieth century stressed the passions of poetry and "feeling" as much as the power of reason. Not until the full impact of Marxism in the 1930's was there a marked return to the worship of reason, science, and technological progress. It was this philosophical legacy of the Old Left, however, that the New Left repudiated, and in doing so the young radicals of the 1960's displayed a deep uncertainty about rationalism, even while invoking the political ideals that had been born in the eighteenth-century Age of Reason. The antagonist still remained bourgeois society, which had disfigured original human nature by its demands for social conformity, economic competition, and sexual repression. Yet, the New Left had few illusions about the liberating power of the historic Enlightenment. At the turn of the century American socialists read Julius Weyland's *Appeal to Reason;* in the 1960's, "reason" was the enemy and the vibrations of "soul" the real test of truth.

If rationalism does not define the mentality of the Left, neither does ideology. In America ideology is a bad word. Supposedly it is a European habit alien to the "pragmatic" wisdom of the American character. This

8 Tom Paine, Revolutionary War patriot and theoretician who believed that man would be liberated through the exercise of simple reason and common sense.

understanding of the term is curious, for it was Marx who first analyzed ideology as a deception and an "illusion." From the Marxist viewpoint, ideology is a rationalization, a verbal "cloak" of ideas behind which true "reality" lies. The American Left, insofar as it has sought to "unmask" ideas like the "laws of the market place" and lay bare the harsh social realities hidden therein, can rightly be described as anti-ideological. But there is another meaning to ideology, one which emerged in the late 1930's when jaded radicals, having lost faith in the "apocalyptic" prophecies of Karl Marx, dismissed Marxism itself as an ideology. Ideology now took on an invidious connotation and came to mean a set of fixed ideas derived from unworkable philosophical systems and unproved scientific laws. Henceforth, to be labeled "ideological" meant that one was hooked on "blueprints," on abstract principles and theoretical doctrines that had nothing to do with reality. In this respect the "end of ideology" anounced by veterans of the Old Left after the Second World War was a way of confessing that they themselves had been out of touch with reality.[7] Yet if the description "ideological" may be applied to the Old Left because of its rigid commitment to Marxist doctrines, this description cannot be applied to the American Left in general. The Lyrical Left of 1913 rose up in revolt against abstract doctrine, embraced a pragmatic socialism that was as open ended as free verse, and proudly heralded itself as conqueror without a creed. Similarly the New Left originally saw itself as the first generation of existential radicals who could live without doctrinal illusions. Ideology was the "brain disease" of the Old Left, taunted some young radicals of the 1960's, and Marxism was its "head trip."

HISTORICAL ROLES

The characteristics most often used to define the Left—the demand for change; political ideals like justice, equality, and democracy; anticapitalism and the tactic of dissent; the mentalities of rationalism and ideology—are either so broad as to include many other political elements or so narrow as to apply to one American Left and not to others. Nevertheless, there are some ways of thinking about the Left that may enable us to approach a historical understanding of its function and role in twentieth-century America.

14

9   American Communist Party members of the 1930's march in a May Day parade, traditional annual demonstration of opposition and of solidarity within the Left.

The Left as Opposition

Without a Right and Center there most likely would be no Left. For the Left is born and takes its shape as an opposition. Since it defines itself by what it rejects as well as what it affirms, the Left is better understood when seen against the background of other political philosophies. In America the two philosophies opposing the Left have been conservatism and liberalism. The conservative Right has generally stood for the primacy of family, religion, authority, and property. The radical Left, in contrast, has called for the liberation of the young, the demystification of religious beliefs, the destruction of traditional authority, and the abolition of private property. The liberal Center—the Left's chief antagonist—has generally been committed to a pluralistic balance of power, an equilibrium of class interests, an ethic of opportunity and achievement, and a realistic vision of human limitations. The Left, in contrast, has demanded the liquidation of institutionalized power and interest politics, the elimination of social classes, the replacement of competitive life with one of fraternal participation and cooperative fulfillment, and unlimited visions of human possibility. Even as a political opposition, however, the Left cannot be understood in terms

15

10   Columbia University students protest the university's acquisition of black ghetto property for expansion. This practice, a tendency in many educational institutions, went largely unquestioned by older generations.

of traditional American politics. The American Left has never, on the national level, been a political party or an effectively organized political movement. Nor has it ever enjoyed political power. Rather, it has been something of a spontaneous moral stance, mercurial and sporadic, suspicious of power and distrustful of politics.

The Left as Negation

Just as the political position of the Left may be identified by its role in opposition, its philosophical temperament may be characterized by its sense of negation. The Left has opposed its enemies by refusing to engage in their practice of politics as the "art of the possible," and it has tried to negate their philosophical foundations by affirming its own vision of an "impossible ideal" as a truth about to be realized.

What do we mean by the concept of negation? In simplest terms, to negate is to deny that the prevailing understanding of reality is valid.[8] Whereas conservatives or liberals may regard war, poverty, or alienation as permanent features of historical reality, the Left regards such phenomena as transitory features of the stages of history—real aspects

16

of immediate historical experience, but not ultimate reality itself. Thus, rather than defending existing conditions, as do conservatives, or reforming them, as do liberals, the Left has sought to transform present society in the hope of realizing "unborn ideals" that transcend historical experience. Unceasing and uncompromising in its attack on present reality, the Left's mentality is fraught with tension. The left-wing intellectual is acutely sensitive to the gap between the real and the ideal, between what *is* and what *ought* to be. The perpetual dilemma of the Left is that it has had to treat the impossible as if it were possible, to accept the huge gap between the real and the ideal and yet struggle to realize the ideal. The philosophical burden the Left has historically assumed would be appreciated by William James (see Chapter 2) as well as by Karl Marx, for the Left recognizes that ideals presently unattainable will never be realized unless they are first articulated as an act of belief.

In attempting to articulate their visionary ideals, and thereby negate the accepted view of reality, different American Lefts have displayed different intellectual resources and temperaments. The Lyrical Left tended at first to rely more upon the regenerating force of culture and the imaginative power of poetry as a means of manifesting "premature truths"; the Old Left saw in the "science" of Marxism a method of historical understanding that would enable man to triumph over the "contradictions" of capitalism; and the New Left at first embraced an existential ethic of moral choice and human commitment as a way of overcoming the paradoxes of alienation.

The Left as a Generational Experience

The concept of negation is also useful in understanding the Left as a generational experience. There is little historical continuity and even less political sympathy among different generations of the American Left. The ex-radicals of the 1930's and the young radicals of the 1960's often spoke past one another whenever they did not shout one another down. The hostility that separated these two Lefts was due not only to different values and attitudes, but also to profoundly different perceptions of reality and history. When the Old Left emerged from the 1930's and underwent the experience of deradicalization, it gradually came to

17

terms with the imperfections of American society, re-embraced American institutions and values, and politically (though not culturally) reconciled itself to existing reality. Certainly not all veterans of the Old Left engaged in what C. Wright Mills called the "great American celebration." Still, we must ask why the New Left saw so clearly the injustices that many members of the Old Left tended to ignore. How did it happen that human minds concerned with the same environment perceived that environment so differently?

It is not enough to say that people of different age groups will see some things differently. How one interprets existing conditions is largely determined by whether one believes they can be fundamentally changed. When the Old Left lost its belief that existing historical reality could be radically transformed, it lost its capacity for negation. To call this behavior of the Old Left a "cop out" is as uncharitable and misleading as to describe the activities of the New Left as a "nihilistic ego trip"—epithets often hurled across the generational barricades. From the perspective of intellectual history, what divided these two radical generations was an implicit debate involving two ponderous questions: What is real? and What is possible? When the Old Left intellectuals abandoned all hope of radical transformation, they tended to accept what existed as the true reality to which all human ideals must conform if they are to be realized. The New Left, innocent of the burden of historical experience, rejected this definition of reality and defiantly invoked a new sense of the possible. Thus the institutions that ex-radicals embraced as real represented to younger radicals the very system that was rejected as unreal because of its alleged irrationality and immorality. Moreover, in denying that war, poverty, racism, and alienation were inherent in the structure of historical reality or in the nature of human existence, the New Left also challenged the concept of reality and human nature that had morally numbed America during the time of the "silent generation" of the 1950's. In so doing the New Left had done for its generation what the Old Left and Lyrical Left had once done for theirs: it articulated a new historical vision, a new sense of reality and possibility that transcended the given state of things, a new consciousness of the negating ideal—that which *ought* to exist, but does not.

11   Art Young, radical cartoonist, comments on the generational experience in 1927. The young flapper says: "Mother, when you were a girl, didn't you find it a bore to be a virgin?"

A generation is not simply a people coexisting in the same time period. What identifies a group as belonging to a particular generation are both a shared perspective on common historical problems and a similar strategy of action taken as a result of that perspective. For the Left in particular, cultural forces and historical crises operate as a "formative experience" upon the mind of a new generation, which in turn shapes its impressions of the world, crystallizes its awakening convictions, and brings into focus its distinct self-consciousness as participants in a common destiny. A radical nucleus of a generation is formed when some young intellectuals or students, as a result of common "destabilizing" experiences, begin to feel, articulate, and defend the identity of certain values and ideals in a society that is indifferent or hostile.[9] Thus, the Lyrical Left rebelled against the philistinism of nineteenth-century Victorian culture and the tawdry machine politics of the two-party system; the Old Left against the political defeatism and cultural despair of the "lost generation" of writers of the 1920's and the "normalcy" politics of the Coolidge era; the New Left against the alienating mass culture of corporate life and the apathetic "consensus" politics of the 1950's. Similarly, the common historical ordeals faced by each Left served to unify radical perspectives and create a generational identity. For the Lyrical Left, those ordeals were the labor struggle, the First World War, the Bolshevik Revolution, the Red Scare, and the socialist-communist split; for the Old Left they were the Depression,

19

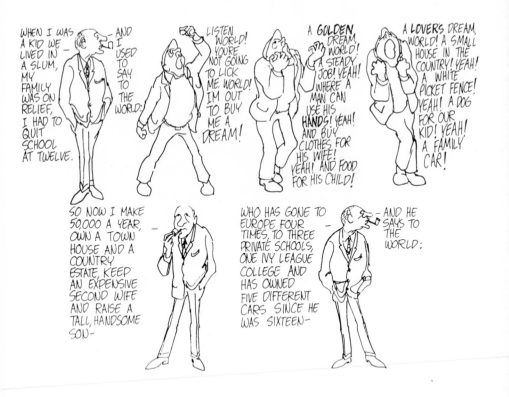

the threat of fascism, the Spanish Civil War, Stalinism and the Moscow trials, and the Russo-German nonaggression pact; for the New Left they were the domestic racial crisis, the wars in Southeast Asia, Cuba, and China, and the politics of confrontation with the resultant fear of repression. These ordeals left deep and lasting impressions on each generation of the twentieth-century American Left. And the very uniqueness of these experiences explains in part why radicals of different generations saw themselves as dissimilar, why they often refuse to listen to one another, why they do not deign to learn from one another.

The Left as an Ally of the Working Class

When we speak of the Left, two different social strata come to mind: the intellectuals and the workers. Historically the Left in America as well as in Europe has attempted to synthesize a single political force

12 Jules Feiffer's ironic comment on two visions of the meaning and purpose of life that often estranged the thirties generation from its children.

out of these two, forging something of an intellectual-worker alliance that would fuse culture and life, thought and action, truth and power. Indeed, one of the most persistent characteristics of the American Left in the twentieth century is this effort of young intellectuals and students to sink their idealistic roots into the material struggles of the working class and to find common cause with the oppressed and exploited. Thus, at first glance it might seem as though the Left could be defined by identifying those social groups it supports and those which it opposes. Using this mode of analysis, the sociologist and political scientist Robert MacIver located the Left as follows:

> The right is always the party sector associated with the interests of the upper or dominant classes, the left with the sector expressive of lower economic or social classes, and the center that of the middle classes. Historically this criterion seems acceptable. The conservative right has de-

21

fended entrenched prerogatives, privileges and powers; the left has attacked them. The right has been more favorable to the aristocratic position, to the hierarchy of birth and wealth; the left has fought for the equalization of advantage or of opportunity, for the claims of the less advantaged. Defense and attack have met, under democratic conditions, not in the name of class but in the name of principle; but the opposing principles have broadly corresponded to the interests of different classes.[10]

There are some difficulties with this class-representation analysis of the Left. Most left-wing intellectuals do not come from the working class, and it is questionable whether their ideals "always" correspond to those of the "lower economic or social classes." On occasion radical writers may have struck a sympathetic response when they addressed

13 Scene at the Homestead strike, early instance of Left-supported working-class assertion.

themselves to the economic concerns of industrial workers. But on such issues as racism, nationalism, culture, religion, and sex they often found themselves in another world. Even the immediate economic interests of the working class can be contrary to the ideals of the Left. At the turn of the century, Left intellectuals failed to instill a spirit of class consciousness in the working class, while labor leaders successfully propounded more conservative principles of opportunity and upward social mobility. Since its cultural ideals are scarcely a replica of the class interests of labor, the Left cannot simply be defined by asserting that it will always be in support of working-class demands.

Why, then, did radical intellectuals in America seek the comradeship of the lower class? One interpretation has been offered by the historian Christopher Lasch. According to Lasch, "the rise of the new radicalism coincides with the emergence of the intellectual as a distinctive social type." Focusing on the changing nature of the social order at the turn of the century, Lasch attempts to show that the "intellectual class . . . is a distinctly modern phenomenon, the product of cultural fragmentation that seems to characterize industrial and post-industrial societies." This cultural disintegration resulted from the decline of tradition, community, and, above all, parental authority, which explains why "the revolt of the intellectuals so often took the form of a rebellion against the conventional family." And this "estrangement" of the intellectuals from the "middle class" and from the "dominant values of American culture" also explains why the intellectual "identified himself with other outcasts and tried to look at the world from their point of view" and to "see society from the bottom up."[11]

Lasch's sociological explanation is richly suggestive but historically limited. The rise of the radical intellectual did not necessarily coincide with the emergence of the "cultural fragmentation" that characterized the social structure of "industrial or post-industrial societies." Well before the full impact of industrialism, the Transcendentalists and utopian reformers of the 1830's and 1840's felt themselves at odds with the prevalent values of American society, and several Brook Farm utopians tried to identify with the plight of the lower class. Moreover, some of the leading intellectuals of the Lyrical Left of 1913 neither broke with their parents nor rebelled against their familial heritage.

23

14 and 15 Social philosopher Thorstein Veblen *(above)* and poet Ezra Pound *(below)*, two alienated intellectuals whose radical critiques of society did not lead to the radical politics of the Left.

Floyd Dell, Max Eastman, and John Reed had the fondest memories of their parents and family upbringing. "When I was sixteen," Reed recalled,

> I went East to a New Jersey boarding school, and then to Harvard College, and afterward to Europe for a year's travel; and my brother followed me through college. We never knew until later how much our mother and father denied themselves that we might go, and how he poured out his life that we might live like rich men's sons. He and mother always gave us more than we asked, in freedom and understanding as well as material things.[12]

Eastman described his father as "kind, reasonable, patient, courageous, sweet-tempered, generous, truthful, just, tempered," and his beloved mother as "heroic" and "saintly."[13] As for the Old Left intellectuals of the Depression, they scarcely questioned the family as a repressive social institution. Indeed, it is not easy to find a direct causal relationship between social origin and political position. Many middle- and upper-class American intellectuals of the First World War generation experienced social estrangement in one form or another, but not all estranged intellectuals became radicals of the Left. One of the most estranged writers of the era, the social philosopher Thorstein Veblen, remained aloof from politics, while another, the poet Ezra Pound, denounced America as a "botched civilization" and went off to Europe to become the rhapsodist of Italian Fascism. Until we understand the mysteries of character and personality, we probably will not know why some alienated intellectuals became Left radicals and others did not. Meanwhile, rather than explain the Left intellectual as a social type, perhaps it is best to try to see the Left as it saw itself—as a new intellectual class with a profoundly radical view of the nature of history and reality.

Notes

[1] Sir Isaiah Berlin, *Two Concepts of Liberty* (Oxford: Clarendon, 1958).

[2] Herbert Marcuse, "Repressive Tolerance," in Herbert Marcuse et al., *A Critique of Pure Tolerance* (Boston: Beacon, 1965), pp. 81–117.

[3] Randolph Bourne, "This Older Generation," *The Atlantic*, CXVI (Sept., 1915), 385–91.

[4] David Caute, *The Left in Europe Since 1789* (London: Weidenfeld and Nicolson, 1966).

[5] Staughton Lynd, *Intellectual Origins of American Radicalism* (New York: Pantheon, 1968).

[6] For a critique of Lynd's argument, see John P. Diggins, "Thoreau, Marx, and the 'Riddle' of Alienation," *Social Research*, XXXIX (Winter, 1972), 571–98.

[7] Daniel Bell, *The End of Ideology: On the Exhaustion of Political Ideas in the Fifties* (New York: The Free Press, 1960); on the conceptual ambiguities surrounding this issue, see John P. Diggins, "Ideology and Pragmatism: Philosophy or Passion?" *American Political Science Review*, LXIV (Sept., 1970), 899–906.

[8] In his classic work, *Ideology and Utopia*, Karl Mannheim first pointed out a crucial epistemological distinction that separates the Right from the Left: the former uses ideology to defend the existing order as real and valid, and the Left projects utopian ideas to challenge that order as false and to direct activity toward undermining it. Since "utopian" is so often used as a term of abuse to deride any new radical idea as a pipedream, it seems more appropriate to use the term "negation." Much of my discussion of this idea is drawn from Leszek Kolakowski's illuminating essay, "The Concept of the Left," in *Toward a Marxist Humanism: Essays on the Left Today* (New York: Grove Press, 1969), pp. 67–83.

[9] Karl Mannheim, "The Problem of Generations," in *Essays on the Sociology of Knowledge* (London: Routledge, 1959).

[10] Robert MacIver, quoted in Seymour Martin Lipset, *Political Man: The Social Bases of Politics* (Garden City, N.Y.: Anchor, 1963), p. 232.

[11] Christopher Lasch, *The New Radicalism in America, 1889–1963: The Intellectual As a Social Type* (New York: Vintage, 1967), pp. ix–xviii.

[12] John Reed, "Almost Thirty" (unpublished manuscript, Houghton Library, Harvard University), p. 8.

[13] Max Eastman, *Enjoyment of Living* (New York: Harper, 1948), pp. 15–26; see also Floyd Dell, *Homecoming: An Autobiography* (New York: Farrar, 1933).

The New 2
Intellectuals

How awful for the world . . . that there are
40,000 revolutionary students in Russia, without a proletariat or even a revolutionary peasantry behind them and with no career before
them except the dilemma: Siberia or abroad—
to western Europe. If there is anything which
might ruin the western European movement,
then it would have been this import of 40,000
more or less educated, ambitious, hungry Russian nihilists; all of them officer candidates
without an army.

Engels to Marx, 1870

To see the Left as an intellectual class is to accept the Left on its own
terms, for it was with this self-image that several young radical writers
and college graduates first attempted to ally themselves with the socialist movement in the United States. The appearance of the first Left of the
twentieth century as an intellectual class raises three important questions: What exactly was meant by "intellectual"? Why did many socialists at first resist the efforts of intellectuals to enter their ranks? Who
were these radical, upper-class intellectuals who were finally hailed as a
vanguard and recognized as the first genuine American Left of the
twentieth century?

THE LEFT INTELLECTUAL

The term "intellectual" first came to be used to describe a group at the time of the Dreyfus affair (1898–1906), when the radical French intellectual community rose to defend the Republic against the reactionary anti-Dreyfusard's. From the beginning, the term conveyed clear political implications: ethically it implied that men of ideas should serve as the authentic conscience of society; socially it described a class of writers, artists, journalists, and professors who felt themselves separated from society; ideologically it suggested that those who chose intellectual life as a vocation should repudiate the interests of their bourgeois class and remain forever independent of the corrupting power of institutions. William James, the first American known to use the term, touched upon some of these implications when he wrote in response to the Dreyfus affair: "We 'intellectuals' in America must all work to keep our precious birthright of individualism and freedom from these institutions [church, army, aristocracy, royalty]. *Every* great institution is perforce a means of corruption—whatever good it may do. Only in the free personal relations is full ideality to be found."[1]

Conflict with Marxian Socialists

Several radical intellectuals who graduated from college between the turn of the century and the First World War tried to find their full ideality in the American socialist movement. They were young writers whose first commitment was to culture, to those elevating pursuits that deepen the mind and heighten the imagination. This commitment created a *mésalliance,* for the Marxist socialists who came to dominate American radicalism after the turn of the century possessed no theory of a cultural class. Indeed, the idea that a revolutionary movement needed an intellectual class appeared almost alien to Marxist theory—or at least to the American version of Marxism that prevailed in the years preceding the First World War. American Marxism was characterized by an optimistic faith in natural science and historical progress. Since history was unfolding rationally according to predetermined "laws," society could be studied through the same empirical methods used in natural science. This deterministic view of history presented an awkward problem for the cultural intellectuals who wanted to become socialists and yet re-

28

main men of ideas. If socialism would develop automatically from the natural laws of history, what role could the radical intellectual perform? If history is determined by economic changes, what role could ideas play in the transformation of society? In the struggle to liberate the working class, Marx saw no crucial function for the moral idealism and cultural criticism of the intellectual class. It is one of the curious ironies of history that Karl Marx, the greatest radical mind of the nineteenth century, developed a theory of history that offered no decisive or central role for the radical mind of the intellectual.[2]

Issues similar to these occupied socialist theorists from the turn of the century to the outbreak of the First World War. In 1900, *The International Socialist Review*, a scholarly journal edited in Chicago by the historian A. M. Simons, published an essay entitled "Socialism and the Intellectuals," by the French writer Paul Lafargue, son-in-law of Karl Marx. Simons and Lafargue warned against the "bourgeois intellectual" who would enter the workers' movement, not as a combatant in the class struggle, but as a *déclassé* "aristocrat" and "mandarin," a "brain worker" who wanted to open the movement to "all amiable exploiters." The volatile Daniel DeLeon, the most militant of American Marxists, took up the attack against the intelligentsia. Stressing the need for working-class unity, DeLeon lashed out at the "pernicious influence" of the

16 Daniel DeLeon, leading American Marxist theoretician, critic, and opponent of emerging middle-class Left intellectuals.

intellectual who "is incapable of learning; of seeing that he joins the Movement, not for the Movement's sake, but for his own." At every critical moment, complained DeLeon, the intellectual betrays the movement, sacrificing its "interests to his own crossed malevolence." This curious attack on intellectuals by intellectuals did not go unanswered. John Spargo, one of the first Americans to write a book on Karl Marx, described the leaders of the anti-intellectual campaign as "unsuccessful 'intellectuals'—lawyers without clients, authors without publishers, professors without chairs, ministers without pulpits." But intellectuals continued to be attacked from both sides of the Left, the radical wing depicting them as dispossessed professionals seeking soft positions in the labor movement, the conservative wing as dangerous adventurers and extremists who joined the movement to overcome the boredom of bourgeois existence. And perhaps both sides could agree with a coal miner who charged that the "radical bourgeois" was more concerned with such goals as free love than with the "stomach ideals" of the workers. Even more disturbing, intellectuals potentially had feet of clay: "They can steal over into the capitalist camp at any time—we can't. They can retire from the firing line—we can't."[3]

Above the crossfire of polemics hovered a deeper philosophical debate —that between materialism and idealism. Many party socialists unsympathetic to intellectuals were steeped in a crude concept of economic determinism and mechanical materialism, a scientific philosophy of history that precluded subjective ideas and creative imagination. The independent radical intellectuals, on the other hand, insisted that their function was to infuse the movement with idealism and theoretical vision, thereby making the implicit claim that they possessed a consciousness that transcended the working class. The intellectuals' case gained a better hearing shortly before the First World War. With the rising prestige of French socialism, which stressed Jean Jaurès's ethical idealism and a radical version of Henri Bergson's "élan vital," the role of moral will and intuition found a place in radical theory. The intellectual could now be regarded as an active and creative force. And if ethical consciousness was a determining influence, perhaps revolutions could originate within the mind, even the mind of the avant-garde intellectual.[4]

Yet by no means had the issue been resolved in 1914 when Robert Rives LaMonte wrote his provocative essay on "The New Intellectuals" in the *New Review,* a theoretical journal of American Marxism. The essay celebrated the appearance of a new radical intelligentsia that emerged just before the war. These young rebels differed from two distinct previous radical types: the eager provincial who, LaMonte said, failed to build a socialist movement because, "sneering" at the doctrine of "scientific socialism," he "contemptuously" dismissed Marxism; and the enthusiastic immigrant student from New York's east side, a "one-book man" who failed because "his intensity of concentration upon Marx deprived him of that broad general culture without which it is impossible to use the Marxian viewpoint and method fruitfully." But the younger radicals, the author pointed out, were free of textual dogmatism, anxious to absorb Nietzsche along with Marx and thus become "steeped in the culture of the day and generation." Still, it was doubtful that the young radicals had successfully resolved the issue of determinism versus freedom and materialism versus idealism. They advocated a "pragmatic" socialism that was "anthropocentric," that placed the "conscious, willing individual" at the center of history. Quoting from a book by one of the young intellectuals, LaMonte noted that what they meant by socialism was not the economic system but "the will, the will to beauty, order, neighbourliness, not infrequently a will to health." Nevertheless, what impressed LaMonte was the free-spirited pragmatism of their "winsome open-mindedness," their "breadth of vision," and their "intellectual and moral receptivity." He thus welcomed the new liberators of the mind: "Hail to the New Intellectuals! May they increase and flourish!"[5] And flourish they did.

Walling, Lippmann, and Eastman

LaMonte had singled out William English Walling, Walter Lippmann, and Max Eastman. These "New Intellectuals" represented a new breed of radical: intellectuals of upper-class sensibilities and lower-class sympathies, original thinkers capable of turning easy answers into harder questions and stimulating new trains of thought, men of action as well as ideas. Walling, a founder of the National Association for the Advancement of Colored People, was one of the few American socialist

17 and 18   William English Walling *(left)* and Walter Lippmann *(right)*, prominent among the New Intellectuals.

The
MASSES
DECEMBER, 1913   10 CENTS

COMING!

' HE STIRRETH UP THE PEOPLE '

JESUS CHRIST
THE WORKINGMAN OF NAZARETH
WILL   SPEAK
AT   BROTHERHOOD   HALL
— SUBJECT —
— THE RIGHTS OF LABOR —

SPECIAL CHRISTMAS NUMBER

19   Cover of the December 1913 issue of *The Masses,* monthly magazine founded by the New Intellectuals.

20   Max Eastman, another of the New Intellectuals, addresses a crowd in Union Square, New York City, in 1917.

intellectuals willing to face squarely the theoretical difficulties of socialism. Lippmann, a brilliant young Harvard graduate who had run as a socialist mayoralty candidate in upstate New York, wrote his first book on political philosophy in 1913 at the remarkable age of twenty-three. Eastman, a handsome, flamboyant poet, a Columbia University philosophy teacher, and an organizer of the early feminist and pacifist movements, was one of the dominant figures in American cultural life between 1913 and 1922. These three intellectuals represented a nucleus of important writers who had joined with other young radicals to publish the *New Review* and *The Masses,* the organs of the first American Left of the twentieth century. Around 1913 many of these writers flocked to New York's Greenwich Village and formed a colony of infidels and iconoclasts who spoke of the coming American "renaissance" and celebrated everything and anything that was new. Here, for a brief moment in American history, cultural rebellion and social revolution seemed to have come together in a thrilling synthesis of art and activism. The radiant illusion was short lived, but while it lasted it gave the first Left its distinct bohemian flavor.

33

THE HISTORICAL CONSCIOUSNESS OF THE LEFT

This Lyrical Left is discussed in a subsequent chapter. At this point it is necessary to say something about the historical consciousness that characterized the Left and distinguished it from other expressions of political and cultural radicalism.

The Role of Dewey and James

Eastman, Lippmann, and Walling had been influenced by various doctrines of European socialism. Their commitment to socialism, however, was conditioned by a deeper commitment to a pragmatic and existential conception of the nature of reality and history. From the philosopher John Dewey, they had learned that knowledge was essentially experimental and that truth was to be realized in practice. As a technique of inquiry, Dewey's philosophy of "instrumentalism" liberated American thought from abstraction and contemplation, making the intellect not a talent to be admired, but a tool to be applied to social problems. Yet Dewey's faith in scientific intelligence and empirical methodology seemed to drain human thought of its emotional currents. Far more congenial to the poetically minded Left intellectuals was the

21   John Dewey about the time of his invitation by the Soviet Union to help set up a public school system there.

22 Pragmatic philosopher William James, whose vision of an "unfinished" reality was particularly congenial to the intellectuals of the Lyrical Left.

thought of William James, a pragmatic philosopher with an existential temperament, a "mystic in love with life," as George Santayana remarked, and one who knew the meaning of "alienation" long before the term became a boring cliché.

No one agonized more over the problem of knowledge and reality than did the young James. In his early years he was struck by a "fear of my own existence" that felt like "a horrible dread at the pit of my stomach." A psychologist interested in the soul and spirit, James later overcame his morbid depression by turning to the mysterious powers of belief. He also brought all abstract philosophical issues together under the immediate phenomenon of "experience": the world may be without ultimate metaphysical meaning, and man may be a creature without ultimate essence; yet in experiencing the world, in the process of expanding his consciousness, man can impose meaning upon it and thereby create his own essence. What counted was will, purpose, and effort. Thus James made the emotions a source of energy that could influence objective reality. He advised a group of Harvard students: "Believe that life *is* worth living, and your belief will help create the fact." James's philosophy enabled the alienated intellectual to overcome scientific skepticism and moral paralysis, for life could now be conceived as an "adventure" that involved "passional decisions" and even a "leap" to faith. After James's classic essay, "The Will to Believe" (1896), it was no longer necessary to struggle over hair-splitting metaphysical squabbles like determinism, for reality was essentially "unfinished" and man was as free as he chose and "willed" to be. Although James was far from a

35

politically minded philosopher, the implications of his thought were profoundly radical: believe that the world can be changed, and your belief will help change it.[6]

For the upper-class intelligentsia Dewey and James played an important role in making intellectual radicalism possible. Their world view eliminated a closed, rational order, a harmonious system in which man must find his proper place in the structure of reality as ordained by God or nature. Nor was history, as the determinists argued, a mere succession of events that proceeded along the plane of natural causation, independent of the desires and will of man. On the contrary, reality was dynamic and unfolding, and man active and creative. It is this conception of historical reality and human nature that Walling conveyed in *The Larger Aspects of Socialism* (1913), where James's idea of poetic imagination and Dewey's idea of social experimentation are combined to present Marxism as a creative adventure as well as a pragmatic science. Lippmann and Eastman shared this view. Lippmann, a former student of James who admired Marx as a demanding thinker who "set the intellectual standards of socialism on the most rigorous intellectual basis he could find," defended Walling when he was criticized by LaMonte for his pragmatic interpretation of Marxism. Lippmann was too skeptical a thinker to accept either pragmatism or Marxism as flawless intellectual propositions. But his brief commitment to socialism was characterized by the Jamesian imperative that one must believe in the historically impossible to overcome the corrosive effects of critical doubt. To those who drew upon history to show that socialism would only replace bourgeois exploitation by proletarian domination, Lippmann replied: "That may be true, but it is no reason for being bullied by it into a tame admission that what has always been must always be. I see no reason for exalting the unconscious failure of other revolutions into deliberate models for the next one."[7]

The Task of Mind

One of the chief characteristics of the historical consciousness of the first Left was its willingness to believe that what "has always been" can be negated, that reality can be acted upon and transformed through conscious human effort. What tended to set left-wing thinkers apart from radical literary innovators like the poet Ezra Pound, or radical disturbers of convention like the journalist H. L. Mencken, was the conviction that the world could be remade by carrying theoretical and moral thought over into the field of practical action. Along with older cultural pessimists like Henry Adams and Mark Twain, the "New Intellectuals" of 1913 also felt estranged from the prevalent values of American society; but whereas the morose historian and the brooding novelist tried to find solace in a lost, mythical past, the younger radicals believed their thoughts could be made useful in contemporary society. Similarly, the Left felt itself linked with the literary bohemians by a common hatred of bourgeois hypocrisy; but, whereas the artists tended to limit themselves to contemplating and expressing esthetic ideas, the Left insisted upon the political actualization of ideas. Finally, the Left shared with the socialists a revulsion against capitalism; but, whereas the "scientific socialists" awaited the unfolding of the objective "laws" of economics, the young rebels were convinced that truth was not so much found or discovered but created and made actual.

All these tendencies fructified in the brilliant mind of Max Eastman, the poet-philosopher of the Lyrical Left. Significantly, liberals and reformers were Eastman's favorite targets. Liberals were "soft-headed idealists" who believed in the virtue of nationalism and the efficacy of class cooperation. Accepting pragmatism but rejecting Marxism, liberals used their "minds to mitigate the subjective impact of unpleasant facts instead of defining the facts with a view to drastic action." Specifically, liberals ruled out the "drastic" weapon of working-class struggle:

> Between revolutionist and reformer there is . . . a flat contradiction of wish, belief, and action. The reformer wishes to procure for the workers their share of the blessings of civilization; he believes in himself and his altruistic oratory; he tries to multiply his kind. The revolutionist wishes the workers to take their blessings of civilization; he believes in them and their organized power; he tries to increase in them the knowledge of their situation and the spirit of class conscious aggression.[8]

Eastman criticized liberals for trying to "mitigate" and "blur" the existence of class conflict, for idealizing the real instead of realizing the ideal, for interpreting existing conditions instead of drastically changing those conditions through the will to believe and the will to act. Putting Marx's notion of "praxis" into verse, Eastman expressed eloquently the idea of negation:

> Mind's task is not to blur the real
> With mimic tints from an ideal
> But to change one into another by an act.[9]

Arising as an opposition to liberalism and conservatism, possessing the will to negate reality, perceiving itself as a new generation with a new historical consciousness of freedom and possibility, the first Left of the twentieth century set out to conquer the world armed, not with a systematic ideology, but with a vague strategy of class conflict and working-class struggle. This strategy confronted the Lyrical Left with a problem that would continue to confound every American Left in the twentieth century—the problem of the proletariat.

Notes

[1] Henry James, ed., *The Letters of William James* (Boston: Atlantic Monthly, 1920), Vol. II, pp. 100–01.

[2] The rise of student radicalism in the 1960's rekindled the debate over young intellectuals that had been first broached by Marxists in the late nineteenth century. See Lewis S. Feuer, *Marx and the Intellectuals: A Set of Post-Ideological Essays* (Garden City, N.Y.: Doubleday, 1969), pp. 53–69; and Shlomo Avineri, "Feuer on Marx and the Intellectuals," *Survey: A Journal of Soviet and East European Studies,* no. 62 (Jan., 1967), 152–55.

[3] Paul Lafargue, "Socialism and the Intellectuals," *The International Socialist Review,* I (Aug. 1, 1900), 84–101; Paul Buhle, "Intellectuals in the Debsian Socialist Party," *Radical America,* IV (Apr., 1970), 35–58; Lewis S. Feuer, "The Political Linguistics of 'Intellectual,'" 1898–1918," *Survey,* no. 78 (Winter, 1971), 156–83.

[4] Jean Jaurès and Paul Lafargue, *Idéalisme et matérialisme dans la conception de l'histoire* (Toulouse, 1895); Charles B. Mitchell,"Bergsonism and Practical Idealism," *New Review,* II (Apr., 1914), 224–27.

[5] Robert Rives LaMonte, "The New Intellectuals," *New Review,* II (Jan., 1914), 35–53.

[6] William James, *Varieties of Religious Experience* (New York: Longmans, 1902), 157; *id., Pragmatism and Other Essays* (New York: Washington Square Press, 1963), pp. 187–213.

[7] William English Walling, "The Pragmatism of Marx and Engels," *New Review,* I (Apr. 5, 1913), 434–39; *ibid.* (Apr. 12, 1913), 464–69; Walter Lippmann, "LaMonte, Walling and Pragmatism," *New Review,* I (Nov., 1913), 907–09; *id., A Preface to Politics* (New York: Charles Kennerly, 1913) pp. 282, 303.

[8] Max Eastman, "Knowledge and Revolution," *The Masses,* IV (Dec., 1912), 1.

[9] Max Eastman, *Reflections on the Failure of Socialism* (New York: Universal Library, 1955), p. 57.

Strangers in the Land 3
The Proletariat
and Marxism

Morally and spiritually I was sickened. I
remembered my intellectuals and idealists,
my unfrocked preachers, broken professors,
and clean-minded class-conscious workingmen, . . . a spiritual paradise of unselfish and
ethical romance. And I saw before me, ever
blazing and burning the Holy Grail. So I
went back to the working class.

Jack London, 1907

Whatever its social or psychological origins, the modern intellectual's
fascination with the working class derives in large part from the doctrines and ideas of Karl Marx. Marx saw the laboring masses as the
vehicle of social transformation because they possessed the sheer weight
of numbers, felt the economic crises more acutely than other classes,
and were strategically located in the industrial system. Moreover, it was
not the intellectuals, but the proletariat that was destined to liberate
mankind: philosophers only interpret the world, the proletariat can
change it. In Marx's theory of knowledge, to think is to act, and to work
and produce is to know the world by laboring upon it and transforming
it. Glorifying work as an activity higher than thought itself, Marx came
close to believing that the proletariat would be able to grasp "the self-

39

awareness adumbrated in the speculations of the philosophers."[1] As the agency of historical consciousness, the proletariat would fulfill its predetermined mission by struggling to emancipate man from capitalist domination, peacefully if possible, violently if necessary.

This chapter is concerned with two questions: Why did the first American Left of the twentieth century fail to find a true revolutionary proletariat in the organized farmer and labor movements? Why did that Left reject the nineteenth-century tradition of American radicalism and turn to Marxism as the true revolutionary ideology?

FARMERS AND INDUSTRIAL WORKERS

In the opening years of the twentieth century the United States was still primarily an agricultural country. Neither backward nor underdeveloped, rural America did not have the volatile peasantry and agrarian anarchism that characterized many countries with revolutionary traditions or tendencies. Yet, toward the end of the nineteenth century the most exciting and powerful expression of radical protest in America came from the farmers' populist movement. Populism had its origins in

23 Karl Marx and his daughter Jenny at about the time of the first publication of his seminal *Capital*.

the sporadic discontent of western and southern growers who began to see themselves as victims of landlords and of exploitation by wealthy interests. Caught between the familiar squeeze of declining commodity prices and rising farm costs, gouged by inequitable rail rates, and harassed by eastern creditors and bankers, the growers struck back by organizing one of the most aggressive political movements of the late nineteenth century. In the early nineties the populist Peoples' Party could control or influence a dozen state legislatures and claim four senators and over fifty congressmen. The programs it advocated made it appear a radical force of the Left. Populists demanded government ownership or regulation of railroads and telegraph systems, lower tariffs, a graduated income tax, control of monopolies, direct election of senators, and low-interest government loans to farmers. Radical proposals of this sort shook the conservative classes everywhere. When the eloquent William Jennings Bryan won the Democratic presidential nomination in 1896 and adopted parts of the populist platform, the urban press headlined prophecies of doom.

Since populism antagonized the industrialists, it aroused the imagination of many young radicals. Several prominent American socialists passed through a populist phase on their way to Marxism; the title of the autobiography of communist William Z. Foster—*From Bryan to Stalin*—reflects this. Yet serious ideological differences existed between populism and socialism. Populists rightly stressed the dangers of concentrated industrial power, but Marxists regarded the farmers' single-minded attacks upon the trusts as a misreading of history. Most Marxists accepted industrial centralization as inevitable and progressive, since business growth and consolidation would produce more industrial workers and tend to drive out the petit entrepreneur, thereby swelling the ranks of the proletariat and setting the stage for revolution. Social and ethnic issues also separated radical intellectuals from populists. Left intellectuals were at home in the cosmopolitan life of the city, whereas southern and western farmers feared the city as alien, parasitical, and subversive to the traditional institutions of family and religion. Although populist leaders cooperated with labor in a few states, and even won the support of the "Colored Alliance," an organization of black field workers in the South, they displayed little under-

24 Early populism and agrarian radicalism in America. A meeting of The Grange in Scott County, Illinois, in the late nineteenth century.

standing of the needs of urban workers and the aspirations of immigrants. Populist monetary policy also alienated the radical Left. Convinced that money was power, populists advocated easy credit and the free coinage of silver in order to alleviate the burden of debts and to challenge the gold standard of eastern bankers. To the socialist Left such programs merely confused the symptom and the cause by equating the "curse of gold" with the crime of capitalism.

The limitations of agrarian radicalism as a potential component of the Left can better be seen in the "contradictions" of populism. Populist leaders desired to destroy the national banking system but preserve local state banks; they attacked industrial property but not private property; they demanded government control of railroads and monopolies but stopped far short of calling for the nationalization of the means of production, which would include the sacrosanct farm itself. Populists and socialists did tend to have a common vocabulary and common targets. Populists matched the Marxist theory of "surplus value" with their own notion of the "labor-cost theory of wealth," thereby juxtaposing the real "producing classes" against the corporate "interests." Yet the populist appeal to the dignity and justice of human toil scarcely

25 Populist William Jennings Bryan at the 1912 Democratic Convention.

echoed Marx's hope of doing away with the "alienated labor" that he saw as a product of capitalism, although one recent historian has maintained that it did.[2] Actually populist values sprang from a traditional Protestant ethic that made hard, honest work the expression of high moral character. Indeed, the influence of that conservative ethic could be seen in the fact that farmers frequently attacked socialism as well as industrial capitalism. Socialism threatened "the love of title deeds to home [which] is inbred among the people," stated one midwesterner. Hence socialism "inevitably destroys all independence of individual action and love of country." Committed to individualism and patriotism, many populists shared the fundamental premises of American capitalism: the "sacredness" of property, the value of opportunity, and the virtue of work. "Socialism would only replace one master by another, the monopolist by the community," declared a journal of the western populists. "All the systems of anarchy and socialism are based upon a supposed quality innate in man which history from the earliest moment of his existence has disproved." Moving from the lessons of history to the principles of psychology, the journal raised the most troubling question of all: "Without individual competition and rivalry

43

what is there to emulate? The answer must inevitably be nothing."[3]

Young radicals who had read Veblen's sociology of rural life knew what the populists wanted to "emulate." For populism ultimately betrayed a love-hate relationship with capitalism wherein the "interests" of Wall Street were opposed in order that the "higher interests" of Main Street might prevail. The acid test was Marxism, and the "inflexible reluctance" of the midwest to tolerate "Marxian ideas," stated the Lyrical literary intellectual Randolph Bourne, revealed "its robust resistance to . . . self knowledge."[4] Steeped in Jeffersonian individualism and Protestant morality, populism could attack capitalism politically but never transcend it intellectually. Since its leitmotif was restoration rather than revolution, populism waxed and waned with the rise and decline of economic grievances.

The Lyrical Left never placed much hope in the farmers, but the failure of industrial workers to produce a radical proletariat raises a question that has troubled radicals and scholars since the turn of the century: Why is the American working class so conservative? If this question could be answered we might better understand why socialism failed in the United States and why the life of each Left has been so feeble and short.

Several answers have been suggested: the existence of the American frontier, which, while it may not have offered a safety valve to the propertyless workers in eastern cities, did keep the labor supply limited (and unemployment low) by slowing the growth of urban populations; America's advanced economic development and national income, which, while grossly maldistributed, enabled Americans to enjoy relative prosperity long before most Europeans; the American labor force, which, while perhaps materially no better off than German workers before the First World War, was characterized by the ethnic heterogeneity of immigrant groups, a factor that hindered development of class identity and promoted the desire of their descendants to exceed the status of their parents and prove themselves "respectable" Americans; and, finally, the fluid nature of America's social structure, which, while not offering a universal "rags to riches" ladder to success, may have offered meaningful low-level mobility. The factor of upward social mobility is crucial, and although the paucity of historical data makes it hazardous to generalize about working-class attitudes, curiosity impels us to speculate. If American workers believed in the capitalist ideology of opportunity and mobility, did those who failed to rise see the cause of their failure as personal inadequacy rather than social inequity and thereby suffer guilt and self-deprecation? On the other hand, if workers remained skeptical of the ideology, why did they fail to develop a radical class consciousness as a means of penetrating the deception? Or were economic opportunity and occupational mobility not myth, but in some measure plausible reality? However these questions will be answered by further research, one fact seems incontestable: the American working class was far from experiencing what Marx called the "increasing misery" of the proletariat—and no one was more aware of this fact than Samuel Gompers.[5]

As President of the American Federation of Labor, Gompers was the bane of the Left. Earlier in the nineteenth century the American labor movement had seemed to offer a radical alternative to the status quo. The militant Knights of Labor, an idealistic fraternity of toilers organized after the Civil War, attempted to forge the unity of all who labored—black and white, women and children, the skilled and un-

26 Samuel Gompers, whose advocacy of immediate and limited material goals as early leader of American trade unionism was bitterly opposed by the socialists.

skilled. This experiment in working-class solidarity soon petered out, and by the end of the century the AFL dominated the labor movement in the United States. Under Gompers' powerful leadership, the AFL concentrated on organizing skilled workers, and its membership grew increasingly elitist and exclusive. In contrast to the Knights' comprehensive reform unionism, the AFL's "pure and simple" trade unionism aimed not so much to liberate man by humanizing the work process, but to secure greater economic gains from management. To machinists, shoemakers, typesetters, and hard-working craftsmen living on the edge of survival, a wage increase was a godsend. But to the left-wing intellectuals, the AFL offered no ideological challenge to capitalism other than demanding more of its profits so that workers could purchase more of its products. Gompersism, as George Bernard Shaw said of trade unionism, was the capitalism of the proletariat.

American socialists attempted to challenge Gompers' leadership. But a key to the weakness of that challenge may be seen in the famous debate in 1914 between Gompers and Morris Hillquit. A Latvian immigrant, Hillquit became one of the chief spokesmen for the philosophy of socialism in America. A leading popularizer of Marxism, he effectively answered the attacks by critics who feared collective ownership as a threat to individual liberty. Yet in his debate with Gompers, Hillquit was reluctant to define an "end" or "ultimate goal" of socialism other than to say that socialists' demands went "further" and "higher" than those of the AFL. The basic difference between socialism and trade unionism was, Hillquit admitted, "a quantitative one—that the Socialist Party wants more than the American Federation of Labor."[6] Such a formulation had serious limitations. Without an enduring ideal toward which labor must struggle, without a theoretical vision that would guide everyday decisions, it was difficult for socialists to check practice against theory and even more difficult for workers to know how to distinguish the "quantitative" promises of socialism from those of capitalism.

Hillquit aside, other socialist intellectuals did hold out for inviolable ideals regardless of the possibility of their realization. In this respect, Gompers may have possessed a better "materialist" grasp of historical forces than even sophisticated Marxists like Daniel DeLeon. Shunning all vague ideals, Gompers believed that "only the concrete and the immediate were material"—higher wages, shorter hours, better working conditions. As Theodore Draper has shrewdly observed: "Whatever success Gompers had, and the Socialists did not have, was scarcely a repudiation of the Marxist emphasis on material interests. It might have indicated the need for American Marxists to take their materialism a little more materialistically."[7] There lay one predicament confronting intellectual radicals: to meet the immediate, material needs of the American working class they ran the risk of settling for less than socialism, which is not so much a demand for "more" as a demand for the humanization of life. Yet the obverse is also true: as long as the socialist-labor dialogue confined itself to material matters, capitalist values would prevail. For a subtle change would take place in America that the Left had not fully anticipated: As Veblen perceived at the time, the United States would pass from a society of producers to a society of buyers and spenders in which the impulse toward "conspicuous consumption" could possibly influence even the working class. Unable to find satisfaction in routine production, the American worker could

27 Morris Hillquit, socialist spokesman who challenged the Gompers view of the role of trade unionism in America.

very well assume that he would find it in burgeoning consumption. Veblen's *The Theory of the Leisure Class* (1899) presented Marxism with a paradox: the United States was a society with a class structure but without any decisive conflict over the very materialistic values that kept the structure intact. For the pervasive "pecuniary canons of taste" would beguile the working class into believing that man finds his fullest happiness not in productive effort but in grasping for the material symbols of status and achievement, for articles like clean and expensive clothing, which show that the wearer does not engage in manual labor. (The fashionable corset, Veblen observed, rendered women physically unfit for work.) As capitalism held out the promise of more and more material goods, American workers could mistake the abolition of scarcity for the abolition of capitalism. Since the boosters of capitalism could claim to have brought about the miracles of abundance, there was danger that America's "proletariat" would accept the ruling class's power and values.

One problem facing the American Left, then, was the problem of consciousness. The fact that a broad class consciousness would emerge in the working class was an article of faith to most Marxist socialists. Gompers had an answer to this eternal dream of the Left. "I told [the socialists] that the *Klassen Bewusztsein* [class consciousness] of which they made so much was not either a fundamental or inherent element, for class consciousness was a mental process shared by all who had imagination." The real sense of workers' solidarity, argued Gompers, was "that primitive force that had its origins in experience only," the gut-emotion of "class feeling" that developed among organized workers who had a common stake in their craft and position. By a strange coincidence Gompers arrived at somewhat the same conclusion Lenin had been propounding in his struggle with his Russian opponents. Lenin, too, maintained that no inherent quality of "socialist consciousness," no revolutionary vision of "what must be done," resided in the workers. Like Gompers, Lenin believed that class consciousness could be appreciated and nurtured only by those capable of understanding "philosophical, historical, and economic theories. . . ." But where Gompers obviously accepted the "primitive force" of "class feeling," Lenin believed socialist theorists must wage a strenuous *"struggle with*

28 Typical corset advertisement of the early 1900's. The emergence of styles of dress that limited the wearer's ability to work was seen by Thorstein Veblen to be symptomatic of the growing disdain for manual labor in the modern industrial society.

elementalness" and combat the workers' tendency toward either acquiescence or blind, rebellious "spontaneity" that would not lead to coherent revolutionary action. Since workers on their own would develop only a "trade union consciousness," the task of instilling true class consciousness was the unique function of the intellectuals.[8]

THE UTOPIAN TRADITION

Lenin was not the first to demonstrate the role of the intellectual in the reformation of society. Indeed, in the mid-nineteenth century Friedrich Engels, colleague of Karl Marx, thought he had discovered "the existing

49

29 Charles Fourier, French socialist whose American disciples
generally accepted his utopian
ideas but shunned the pansexu-
al aspects of his doctrine.

practice of communism" in various American communities like the
"one at Brook Farm, Massachusetts, where fifty members and thirty
pupils live on about 200 acres, and have founded a distinguished school
under the leadership of a Unitarian preacher, G. Ripley."[9]

In the 1830's and 1840's America spawned a number of small socialist
communes—early experiments in what a later generation would call
"countercultures." The utopian colonies were headed by an odd mix-
ture of spiritualists and sensualists: Christian communists like the
Shaker Mother Ann, who called upon her followers to withdraw from
the polluted world of the flesh and practice celibacy in order to prepare
for the Day of Judgment; secular communists like John Humphrey
Noyes, who advocated the "complex marriage" system of free love in
order to realize the laws of physical and spiritual nature. Many intellectuals and utopians believed, with the French socialist Charles
Fourier, that modern society had distorted original human nature.
Emerson, an admirer of Fourier, best described the fragmentation of the
self: "The state of society is one in which the members have suffered
amputation from the trunk, and strut about as so many walking mon-

sters,—a good finger, a neck, a stomach, an elbow, but never a man."
Fourier's solution was to liberate the "passions" in order to allow the
natural force of "attraction" to govern human behavior. Thus, since
man is as attracted to different objects of desire as he is to different objects of labor, he should be tied down to neither the delight of a single
woman nor the drudgery of a single job. Although Fourier's American
followers (the Associationists) shied away from his pansexualism,
utopians like George Ripley believed that the release of passion "will
call forth, as from a well-tuned instrument, all those exquisite modula-
tions of feeling and intellect, which were aptly termed by Plato, the
'music of his being.'"[10]

Pre–Civil War utopian socialism elicited the enthusiastic response
of many intellectuals, and it influenced a wide variety of campaigns for
educational reform, women's rights, pacifism, and the abolition of
slavery. Significantly, the romantic utopians were the first generation
of American intellectuals to try to integrate socialism with culture, to
unify the life of work with the life of mind, and, in Ripley's words,
"insure a more natural union between intellectual and manual labor
than now exists; to combine the thinker and the worker, as far as possible, in the same individual." Utopians as well as Transcendentalists
believed that only when this fusion of culture and social regeneration
took place could man become truly conscious of his essence and realize
what Emerson called "a perfect unfolding of individual nature." The
first issue of Brook Farm's *The Harbinger* passionately stated this theme.
After discussing literature, painting, music, sculpture, architecture,
drama, "and all arts which seek the Good, by way of the Beautiful,"
the editorial concluded:

> We shall suffer no attachment to literature, no taste for abstract discussion,
> no love of purely intellectual theories, to seduce us from our devotion to the
> cause of the oppressed, the down-trodden, the insulted and injured masses
> of our fellow men. Every pulsation of our being vibrates in sympathy with
> the wrongs of the toiling millions, and every wise effort for their speedy
> enfranchisement will find in us resolute and indomitable advocates. If any
> imagine from the literary tone of the preceding remarks, that we are indif-
> ferent to the radical movement for the benefit of the masses, which is the
> crowning glory of the nineteenth century, they will soon discover their
> egregious mistake. To that movement, consecrated by religious principle,

sustained by an awful sense of justice, and cheered by the brightest hopes of future good, all our powers, talents, and attainments are devoted. We look for an audience among the refined and educated circles, to which the character of our paper will win way; but we shall also be read by the swart and sweaty artisan; the laborer will find in us another champion; and many hearts, struggling with the secret hope which no weight or care and toil can entirely suppress, will pour on us their benedictions as we labor for the equal rights of All.[11]

The utopian impulse also infused the writings of late nineteenth-century thinkers. In Henry George's *Progress and Poverty*, Edward Bellamy's *Looking Backward*, and William Dean Howells' *A Traveler from Altruria*, Americans could find schemes for redistributing non-productive wealth (unearned income) and visions of a future world of social felicity. Together with muckraking journalists and progressive scholars, utopian novelists subjected America to a ferment of social criticism that effectively exposed the injustices of capitalism and the power of the business class. Moreover, unlike the populists and trade unionists, the utopians consciously sought to alter the conditions of work and the quality of life. Nevertheless, despite its humane impulses and enormous popularity, the whole tradition of utopian socialism seemed inadequate to most radicals of the twentieth century.

As models of social conscience, the pre–Civil War utopian communes offered a mirror of self-criticism and a mechanism of escape. But as movements for social change, they produced little of enduring value. Looking back, later generations of radicals would claim that the romantic communitarians failed because they lacked an understanding of economics and a commitment to politics. Setting up fragile enclaves in a brave but innocent attempt to escape the grasping paws of society, utopians assumed they could insulate their communities from the ubiquitous pressures of capitalism. Shunning institutions such as political parties, labor organizations, the law, the church, and the professions, they disengaged themselves from political life. Hopelessly naive about the nature of power ("power ceases in the instant of repose"—Emerson), the Transcendentalists in particular appeared to be formulating useless esthetic solutions to pressing social problems.

Late-nineteenth-century utopians also seemed to have no grasp of economic realities. Approaching socialism as an ethical force, the in-

30 and 31   William Dean Howells *(left)* and Edward Bellamy *(right)*, influential turn-of-the-century novelists who advocated cooperative community but rejected "foreign" socialism.

evitable result of moral progress, many utopians believed they could solicit from men of power the funds with which to build pastures of cooperation within a jungle of competition. Moreover, the utopians had no direct ties to the unorganized and unskilled workers. Though deeply moved by the plight of industrial workers, novelists like Bellamy and Howells were more concerned with the devastating impact of competitive capitalism upon traditional values. Both writers wanted to replace rampant individualism with some version of the cooperative community, and also to keep the virtues of the country safe from corruption by a "foreign" socialism that, in Bellamy's telling words, "smells to the average American of petroleum, suggests the red flag, and all manner of sexual novelties, and an abusive tone about God and religion, which in this country we at least treat with decent respect." This concern for the moral health of the traditional American character linked the two (pre– and post–Civil War) generations of utopian socialists. Defending Fourierism, the journalist Horace Greeley spoke of the need for "education and training," which will lead men to the habits of "Industry, Virtue, Self-Respect, instead of those which naturally lead to Idleness, Dissipation, Vice and Debasement." The politics of middle-class self-preservation, utopian socialism was an attempt to reform the circumstances of economic life in order better to affirm the principles of moral life. Humane, civilized, sincere, genteel, proper, and upright, reform socialism appeared to younger radicals to be the false consciousness of the "starched collar" class.[12]

53

Few members of the Left could find an inspiring political vision in traditional nineteenth-century liberalism and radicalism. Organized farmers and industrial workers never constituted a revolutionary proletariat; utopians never questioned the sanctity of private property; liberals never took up the strategy of class struggle; and humanitarian reformers could never transcend a genteel legacy of polite idealism. Yet there remained one doctrine that supposedly would fill all these needs — Marxism.

THE MARXIST BACKGROUND

The doctrines of Marx were first brought to America by immigrants who fled Germany after the ill-fated uprisings of 1848. Steeped in the problems of class consciousness, German-American Marxists like Joseph Weydemeyer and Friedrich Sorge opposed utopianism as an idle dream completely out of touch with immigrant and proletarian life. The German leaders also organized American branches of the International Workingmen's Association, the First International, which was established in London with the support of Karl Marx. A second generation of German immigrants brought with them the ideas of the founder of German social democracy, Ferdinand Lassalle. Later in the century, as successive waves of Italian, Jewish, and east European immigrants arrived, and the labor struggle in the United States grew more intense, American socialism took on a variety of expressions, including anarchism and syndicalism. These groups divided not over the goal of socialism but over how to achieve it.

Drastically reduced, the arguments revolved around three issues. The first was the argument over politics versus economics. Although positions were never clear and consistent, in general the Lassalleans believed workers and intellectuals must win over the state through political activity. The Marxists, in contrast, maintained that economic struggle through union organization took precedence over electoral politics.

The second issue, involving the pace and nature of historical change, divided the gradualists from the extremists. The right-wing socialists believed the goals of Marx could be realized step-by-step through piecemeal changes, while the left wing held out for an almost apocalyptic

32 and 33 Ferdinand Lassalle *(right),* founder of German social democracy, whose ideas were brought to America in the late-nineteenth century by the second wave of German immigrants. Marxist doctrine had arrived with the first wave mid-century. *(below)* A membership card in the American branch of the International Working Men's Association, founded by its German leaders. Karl Marx's signature as corresponding secretary for the German branch may be seen second from the bottom on the left.

34 Victor Berger, leader of the right wing of the Socialist Party in the controversy over how to establish socialism in America.

leap to socialism. Hence the left wing castigated the palliative reforms sponsored by progressives, claiming that socialism could not be legislated into existence until capitalism was abolished. Similarly, on the issue of trade unionism, the left wing advocated setting up organizations to rival established unions, even though the tactic of "dual unionism" jeopardized efforts at unifying the labor movement, and the right wing advocated entering established unions and "boring from within" in order to educate the workers to socialism. The chief theoretical spokesman for the left wing was Daniel DeLeon, who was dubbed an *"impossibiliste"* by his opponents because of his scorn for immediate programs. The chief practical spokesman for the right wing was Victor Berger, the first American socialist elected to Congress. Their disagreements represented something of a pale repetition of the intense dialogue over "orthodoxy" versus "revisionism" that had occupied the international socialist movement in Europe. DeLeon adhered to the traditional version of class struggle and the triumph of the proletariat, while Berger tried to adapt Marxist principles to American conditions. One saw the birth of socialism in the revolutionary power of the workers, the other in the evolutionary reforms of the government. Moderates accused DeLeon of indulging in revolutionary fantasy, while militants accused Berger of subscribing to an evolutionary fallacy.

The third dispute among socialists arose over the use of violence. Contrary to the myth of peaceful and orderly progress, the United States had been the scene of one of the most ravaging social struggles in the western world. Between 1881 and 1906 there occurred some 30,000 strikes and lockouts, affecting almost 200,000 businesses and over 9½ million workers. From the coal mines of Pennsylvania, where Irish Molly Maguires would methodically murder the management's police spies, to the mine fields of Colorado, where management hired state authorities to terrorize and lynch migrant coal workers, class warfare became a daily reality. After Chicago's famous Haymarket Riot of 1886 socialists disagreed sharply over the tactic of violence. Violence was associated with the idea of anarchism, a simple and yet complex doctrine opposed to all forms of authority and coercion, what Max Nomad has called an elusive "political daydream" of total statelessness and

35   Eleven men, described in a contemporary news account as "the last of the Molly Maguires," march to their execution at Pottsville, Pennsylvania, in 1877.

classlessness. Psychologically as well as politically, anarchist terrorism reflected the utter hopelessness and desperation of the disinherited. By the time of the First World War six chiefs of state had been assassinated in the name of anarchism, including in America, President William McKinley.

There were thousands of anarchists among the Italian-American followers of Enrico Malatesta and the German-American disciples of Johann Most. What troubled the American labor movement, however, was not the sporadic deeds of violence by isolated foreign terrorists, but the sustained doctrine of class warfare of the Industrial Workers of the World. The IWW sprouted in the western states mainly among unorganized, seminomadic lumbermen and miners. The Wobblies, as they

36 Cover of a book giving a contemporary account of the Haymarket Riot trial in 1886. The unsympathetic depiction of anarchists is by Art Young, who bitterly regretted it when he later became a prominent radical cartoonist.

37 A sympathy demonstration for Wobbly agitator Carlo Tresca, on trial at the time (1916) for syndicalist activity.

were called, were tough, boisterous, and defiant. Appropriately, their songs have become part of the idiom of radical folk music, their courageous exploits legendary in the annals of the American Left. A grand brotherhood of drifting hoboes and daring heroes, the Wobblies had more than their share of political martyrs: Wesley Everest, a Northwestern lumberman riddled with bullets by the American Legion after one true patriot castrated him; Carlo Tresca, a colorful agitator gunned down by an unknown political assassin; Joe Hill, a Utah construction worker arrested on a spurious murder charge, who exclaimed while facing a firing squad, "Don't mourn for me. Organize!" Occasionally the IWW organized as many as 30,000 workers; and, in 1912, during the height of its fame, won a dramatic, long-fought textile strike in Lawrence, Massachusetts. The Wobblies believed in syndicalism, originally a French doctrine that held that completely autonomous workers' unions (or syndicates) could lead the masses to socialism. Because of their great faith in the spontaneous, creative character of the proletariat, 59 syndicalists were often at odds with Marxists, who had less faith in the untutored political consciousness of the workers.

What disturbed American socialists was not so much the European issue of "spontaneity" versus "consciousness" as the tactics employed by the IWW. The tactics were a variation on the anarcho-syndicalist theme of "propaganda by the deed": "direct action," "sabotage," and the magic of the "general strike," which supposedly would bring down all authority in a single blow. Yet the Wobblies' use of violence has been greatly exaggerated. Wobblies were convinced that power comes from the barrel of a gun, but they also knew that the ruling class possessed more guns. Although they occasionally resorted to Winchester rifles or dynamite sticks to defend themselves or to retaliate, seldom did Wobblies as an organization use violence as a strategic weapon, and rarely did their leaders really believe—as opposed to the rhetorical bombast of their declarations—that violence alone could lead to power. "I, for one," Wobbly leader Bill Haywood remarked during the Lawrence strike, "have turned my back on violence. It wins nothing. When we strike now, we strike with our hands in our pockets. . . . Pure strength lies in the overwhelming power of numbers."[13] Nevertheless, the issue was fiercely debated at various socialist conferences; and in 1912 the rising tension between the socialists and the syndicalists came to a head when the Socialist Party amended its constitution to prohibit the use of "sabotage." The repudiation of violence made socialism more respectable, but the expulsion of the IWW from the SP made Wobblyism more attractive to the Left in its fight against respectability.

Despite the factionalism, socialism grew rapidly after the turn of the century. In 1901 the newly formed Socialist Party broadened the base of the movement under the inspiring leadership of Eugene Debs. Between 1902 and 1912 the SP's membership grew from 10,000 to 118,000, and its electoral power from 95,000 to the nearly 900,000 votes that Debs gathered as presidential candidate in 1912. During this period it could claim one congressman, 56 mayors, 160 councilmen, and 145 aldermen. The socialist press in America circulated 5 English and 8 foreign-language dailies, 262 English and 36 foreign-language weeklies, and 10 English and 2 foreign-language monthlies. Several developments account for the dramatic rise of American socialism during its "golden

We Have Fed You all A Thousand Years

Poem by an unknown Proletarian
Music by Rudolph Von Liebich--
Pub. by I·W·W· Educational Bureau
Chicago, U·S·A

38   Cover of sheet music distributed by the IWW in 1918.

39 and 40 *(above)* Wobbly leader Big Bill Haywood heads a parade in Lawrence, Massachusetts, in support of the crucial textile strike there. *(below)* Troops hold workers in check at a demonstration during the strike.

years" (roughly 1902–1912): the absorption of populist elements, particularly after 1910 when the SP reversed its 1908 resolution calling for nationalization of farm land; the influx of immigrants and the SP's policy of ethnic pluralism, which allowed Italians, Jews, Germans, Poles, Hungarians, Slavs, Slovaks, and Finns to establish autonomous branches; and the increasing prestige of European socialist parties, some of which appeared to be on the verge of securing an absolute parliamentary majority before the First World War.

Historians differ over when the SP began its decline. According to James Weinstein, the expulsion of the syndicalist Left in 1912 did not impair the growth of socialism, which continued to win the political vote of urban ethnic groups, radical intellectuals, and some middle-class elements discontented with the Democratic and Republican parties. As the research of John Laslett shows, however, the SP lost the support of many important trade unionists like the brewery, shoe, garment, machinist, and mine workers, who began to align with the Democratic party in support of the social and labor reforms of the Wilson administration.[14] Whatever the reasons for the rise and decline of American socialism, its history included some of the most towering figures in twentieth-century American radicalism. Three deserve special mention.

THREE LEADERS IN AMERICAN SOCIALISM

Debs

Most magnetic was Eugene Debs. Straight from the Indiana heartland of America, lanky and bald, a forehead weighted with worry and cheeks crinkled with laughter, Debs was the symbol of integrity. His life history reads almost like a socialist morality tale. At work on the railroads at the age of fifteen, he later gave up stoking locomotives to organize the American Railway Union. In 1893 his union won a crucial strike against James J. Hill's powerful Great Northern Railroad; but instead of following in Gompers' footsteps Debs then used his organizing talents to "eliminate the aristocracy of labor," to try to open up the union movement to all workers. In his early years he had been deeply stirred by the writings of Bellamy and George and later by the speeches

63

41 and 42 *(above)* A campaign poster for Eugene V. Debs and Ben Hanford, Social-ist Party candiates for president and vice president, in 1904. *(facing page)* On the campaign trail in 1904, Debs addresses a crowd at a railroad siding. During his 1920 campaign (conducted from a jail cell) he won almost a million votes.

of Bryan. He also read Marx while serving a prison term for his activi-ties in the bloody Pullman strike of 1894. Debs often recalled the gov-ernment's intervention in that strike as his conversion experience: "At this juncture there were delivered, from wholly unexpected quarters, a quick succession of blows that blinded me for an instant and then my eyes opened—and in the gleam of every bayonet and the flash of every rifle *the class struggle revealed itself.*" Actually Debs' conversion to socialism was much less melodramatic, for despite the Pullman experi-ence he kept faith in democratic reformism until the populist debacle of 1896. Thereafter he entered the SP and emerged as its titular head for almost twenty years. As late as 1920, once again in jail, this time for alleged antiwar propaganda, he drew nearly one million votes as the SP's presidential candidate. Debs had the martyr's charisma, but he also possessed tremendous oratorical power, a "sort of gusty rhetoric," wrote Dos Passos, that made workers "want the world he wanted, a world brothers might own where everybody would split even. . . ." "His tongue," recalled Eastman, "would dwell upon a *the* or an *and* with a

64

kind of earnest affection for the humble that threw the whole rhythm of his sentence out of conventional mold, and made each one seem a special creation of the moment." Although Debs tried to remain above ideological battles, occasionally he criticized the SP's two extreme wings. Chiding "the spirit of bourgeois reform" on the Right, he insisted that "voting for socialism is not socialism any more than a menu is a meal"; opposing the saboteur rhetoric of the syndicalist Left, he maintained that "American workers are law-abiding and no amount of sneering or derision will alter the fact." Debs had his party enemies, but to the Left in general he was a "poet," a "saint," the "sweetest strongman," and a "lover of mankind."[15]

DeLeon

While Debs became the missionary of American socialism, Daniel DeLeon became its metaphysician. DeLeon was an impressive figure. His massive head with its piercing black eyes and carefully trimmed white beard seemed precariously balanced on his short neck and nar-

65

row shoulders. An educated scholar and masterful theoretician, he seemed to carry the whole blueprint for revolution in his brain. After the bolshevik uprising in 1917, the Lyrical radical John Reed, back from Russia, reportedly told his American comrades that Lenin was a "great admirer of Daniel DeLeon" and regarded him as "the only one who had added anything to socialist thought since Marx."[16] Although the story may be apocryphal,[17] Lenin and DeLeon did have much in common. Studying the same developments after the turn of the century, they wrestled with similar problems: the strategy of party organization and control of its press, the "bourgeoisification" of the workers, and the effect of imperialism on the coming revolution. As did Lenin, DeLeon faced the crucial problem of the road to power. Should socialists overthrow the existing order through the efficacy of the ballot (Lassalleans), through the leadership of a mass party (Marxists), or through the economic struggle of radical industrial unions (syndicalists)?

In theory DeLeon attempted a formulation that would reconcile all sides: the SP would be voted peacefully into power, but once established would liquidate itself and turn over the administration of the state to the workers themselves—a foreshadowing of Lenin's *State and Revolution*. In practice, DeLeon was far to the Left of the Debsian socialists and the reformists. Nothing was more repugnant to DeLeon than the revisionist argument that "the movement is everything, the goal nothing." A movement without a clearly defined goal could only secure piecemeal reforms that would leave the structure of capitalist power intact. DeLeon could tolerate economic reforms only if they were accompanied by sustained revolutionary consciousness. What he feared most was Gompersism—the corruption of the working class by bourgeois values and comforts. Ultimately he placed his faith in revolutionary industrial unions that would educate workers and cultivate their class consciousness. Organized like syndicates, the unions would be led by a dedicated cadre.

In all revolutionary movements, as in the storming of fortresses, the thing depends upon the head of the column—upon that minority that is so intense in its convictions, so soundly based in its principles, so determined in its actions, that it carries the masses with it, storms the breastworks and captures the fort.[18]

Haywood

DeLeon's finely spun theories made socialism appear as the perfection of an idea. The socialism of Big Bill Haywood, in contrast, symbolized the beauty of deed and the power of action. Haywood captured the Lyrical Left's imagination, for he came as close as any radical to embodying the proletarian-intellectual, a workingman whose mind and conscience transcends his condition and thereby makes him an articulate spokesman for those who labor with their hands. Haywood was born in a boarding house in Salt Lake City in 1869. As a youth he worked as a bellhop, a messenger boy, and an usher; by age fifteen he was hefting a pick and shovel as a hardrock miner in Nevada, outfitted with "overalls, a jumper, a blue shirt, mining boots, two pairs of blankets, a set of chessmen, boxing gloves and a big lunch of plum pudding his mother fixed for him," wrote Dos Passos. Restless and footloose, he wandered from town to town, working the mines by day and sampling the saloons and brothels by night. He came to know the West not as a land of opportunity but as a brutal terrain for class warfare in which the conflict between labor and capital was irrepressible. In the late nineties he joined the Western Federation of Miners and rose rapidly as an effective union organizer and strike tactician. Shortly afterwards he joined the IWW, and in 1905, during a protracted industrial war in the Colorado coal fields, Haywood and two other union men were kidnapped by Pinkerton agents and brought to Boise to be tried for complicity in the murder of Governor Frank Staunnerberg of Idaho. The entire labor movement came to their defense, and after the great criminal lawyer Clarence Darrow won their acquittal, Haywood became a national figure and a confirmed revolutionary. "Those of us who are in jail," Haywood later wrote to fellow socialists, "those of us who have been in jail—all of us who are willing to go to jail. . . . We are the Revolution!"19

A broad-shouldered man, over six feet tall, with a dark mat of hair and a black patch over a maimed right eye, Haywood seemed the *élan vital* of the wretched of the earth. The British socialist J. Ramsey MacDonald perceived in him the embodiment of Sorel's revolutionary will, "a bundle of primitive instincts, a master of direct statement. . . . I saw him addressing a crowd in England, and there his crude appeals moved his listeners to wild applause. He made them see things, and their hearts bounded to be up and doing."[20] Haywood could move the intellectual Left in much the same way, and when the SP adopted its antisabotage resolution in 1912 and expelled Haywood the following year, several radical intellectuals sided with "Comrade Haywood." By that time Haywood himself had repudiated violence, but the actions of the socialists indicated no understanding of the needs of helpless miners and lumbermen who moved too often to become registered voters. Haywood, the "Polyphemus from the raw mining camps of the West [who] dedicated himself to the organization of the unskilled, the poverty stricken and forgotten workers," symbolized the real poverty and suffering that the intellectuals had never known. He also appealed to the intelligentsia because he seemed to be a poet of the proletariat, the harbinger of a new socialist culture. In Max Eastman's novel *Venture*, Haywood addresses a salon of America's *literati*. After explaining why there can be no art for the Pittsburgh steel worker, he expounds the nature of a true working-class culture:

> "Not only is art impossible to such a man," he said, "but life is impossible. He does not live. He just works. He does the work that enables you to live. He does the work that enables you to enjoy art, and to make it, and to have a nice meeting like this and talk it over."
> Bill used "nice" without irony: he meant it.
> "The only problem, then, about proletarian art," he continued, "is how to make it possible, how to make life possible to the proletariat. In solving that problem we should be glad of your understanding, but we don't ask your help. We are going to solve it at your expense. Since you have got life, and we have got nothing but work, we are going to take our share of life away from you, and put you to work."
> ". . . When we stop fighting each other—for wages of existence on one side, and for unnecessary luxury on the other—then perhaps we shall all become human beings and surprise ourselves with the beautiful things we do and make on the earth. Then perhaps there will be civilization and a civilized art. But there is no use putting up pretense now. The important thing . . . is that our side, the workers, should fight without mercy and win. There is no home for humanity anywhere else."[21]

By and large American socialism was a movement not of, but on behalf of the working class. Although it assumed to speak for the worker and to articulate his needs, the doctrines and tactics had been developed by intellectuals and party leaders. The Wobblies, the embodiment of a working class that spoke for itself and struggled for its own class interests, gave the Left its opportunity to reconcile the aristocracy of intelligence with the nobility of labor. Whereas the earlier Brook Farm utopians hoped that the "swart and sweaty" laborers would rise to culture, the New Intellectuals of 1913 were willing to sit at the feet of Haywood, the authentic voice of a genuine American proletariat, while he expounded the creation of a new and superior culture by the working class. Eastman's image of the Wobbly leader may have been more romantic than real, and likewise the Left's need to believe in a revolutionary proletariat may have been nurtured more by faith than by fact. As the agency of historical transformation, as the ascending class that enables the radical intellectual to maintain a dynamic contact with the masses, the idea of the proletariat lives and dies in the mind of the Left.

Notes

[1] Maurice Merleau-Ponty, quoted in Raymond Aron, "The Myth of the Proletariat," in *The Opium of the Intellectuals* (New York: Norton, 1962), pp. 66–93.

[2] Norman Pollack, *The Populist Response to Industrial America* (New York: Norton, 1962), pp. 68–84.

[3] James B. Webster, "A Farmer's Criticism of the Socialist Party," *The International Socialist Review*, II (May, 1902), 769–73; Howard H. Quint, *The Forging of American Socialism* (Indianapolis: Bobbs-Merrill, 1953), p. 211.

[4] Thorstein Veblen, "The Independent Farmer," and "The Country Town," in *The Portable Veblen*, ed. Max Lerner (New York: Viking, 1948), pp. 395–430; Randolph Bourne, "A Mirror of the Middle West," in *The History of a Literary Radical and Other Papers* (New York: S. A. Russell, 1956), p. 292.

[5] George G. S. Murphy and Arnold Zellner, "Sequential Growth, the Labor-Safety-Valve Doctrine, and the Development of American Unionism," in *Turner and the Sociology of the Frontier*, eds. Richard Hofstadter and Seymour Martin Lipset (New York: Basic Books, 1968), pp. 201–24; Selig Perlman, *A Theory of the Labor Movement* (New York: Macmillan, 1949); Stephen Thernstrom, *Poverty and Progress: Social Mobility in a Nineteenth Century City* (New York: Atheneum, 1970); for an example of the diverse conclusions reached by contemporary scholars studying the mobility question, see Stephen Thernstrom and Richard Sennett, eds., *Nineteenth-Century Cities: Essays in the New Urban History* (New Haven, Conn.: Yale Univ. Press, 1969).

[6] "Hillquit versus Gompers," in *Socialism in America: From the Shakers to the Third International: A Documentary History*, ed. Albert Fried (Garden City, N.Y.: Doubleday, 1970), pp. 471–95.

[7] Theodore Draper, *The Roots of American Communism*, (New York: Viking, 1963), p. 29.

[8] Samuel Gompers, quoted in Daniel Bell, *Marxian Socialism in the United States* (Princeton, N.J.: Princeton Univ. Press, 1967), p. 43; V. I. Lenin, *What Is to Be Done?* (New York: International Publishers, 1929).

[9] Friedrich Engels, quoted in Lewis S. Feuer, "The Alienated Americans and Their Influence on Marx and Engels," in *Marx and the Intellectuals*, p. 171.

[10] Ralph Waldo Emerson, "The American Scholar," in *The Portable Emerson*, ed. Mark Van Doren (New York: Viking, 1946), p. 24; Charles Crowe, *George Ripley: Transcendentalist and Utopian Socialist* (Athens: Univ. of Georgia Press, 1967), p. 173.

[11] *The Harbinger* editorial, in Fried, *Socialism in America*, pp. 161–65; see also John L. Thomas, "Romantic Reform in America, 1815–1865," *American Quarterly*, XVII (Winter, 1965), 656–81.

[12] Edward Bellamy, quoted in Daniel Aaron, *Men of Good Hope* (New York: Oxford Univ. Press, 1951), p. 112; Horace Greeley, "Association Discussed" (1847), in Fried, pp. 149–60; Max Eastman, "Concerning an Idealism," *The Masses*, IV (July, 1913), 1.

[13] Bill Haywood, quoted in Melvyn Dubofsky, *We Shall Be All: A History of the Industrial Workers of the World* (Chicago: Quadrangle, 1969), p. 161.

[14] James Weinstein, *The Decline of Socialism in America 1912–1925* (New York: Monthly Reviews, 1967); John H. M. Laslett, *Labor and the Left: A Study of Socialist and Radical Influences on the American Labor Movement, 1881–1924* (New York: Basic Books, 1970).

[15] Eugene Debs, "Why I Became a Socialist," in *Debs: His Life Writings and Speeches* (Chicago, 1908), p. 82; John Dos Passos, *The 42nd Parallel* (New York: Random House, 1937), p. 26; Max Eastman, *Love and Revolution: My Journey Through an Epoch* (New York: Random House, 1964), p. 114.

[16] John Reed, quoted in Charles A. Madison, *Critics and Crusaders* (New York: Holt, 1947), p. 470.

[17] Max Eastman, "The S.L.P.," *The Class Struggle*, III (Aug., 1919), 304–06; Robert Miner to Eastman, April 20, 1919, Eastman mss, Lilly Library, Indiana University, Bloomington, Ind.

[18] Daniel DeLeon, quoted in Fried, p. 194; see also Louis Fraina, "Daniel DeLeon," *New Review*, II (July, 1914), 390–99.

[19] Dos Passos, *42nd Parallel*, p. 94; William D. Haywood, "The Fighting IWW," *The International Socialist Review*, XIII (Sept., 1912), 247.

[20] J. Ramsey MacDonald, quoted in Melvyn Dubofsky, "The Radicalism of the Dispossessed: William Haywood and the IWW," in *Dissent: Explorations in the History of American Radicalism*, ed. Alfred Young (DeKalb: Northern Illinois Univ. Press, 1968), p. 177.

[21] Bill Haywood, and references to him, quoted in Daniel Aaron, *Writers on the Left: Episodes in American Literary Communism* (New York: Harcourt, 1961), pp. 14, 16–17.

part two

HISTORY

The Lyrical Left 4

When I was up at Columbia University, one of the most unforgettable and most glamorous experiences I recall in my student life was the first lecture I heard by Max Eastman before the Socialist Study Club. He came before us then as the fair-haired apostle of the new poetry, the knight errant of a new and rebellious generation, the man who was making his dreams come true—as poet, as thinker, as editor, as teacher, as psychologist, as philosopher, as a yea-sayer of the joy and adventure of living in the fullest and richest sense of the word. Even then Max was already a glamorous, exciting figure in the world of letters and in the world of adventure. Life was bursting in all its radiance all around him. For him existence was a fight, a song, a revolution, a poem, an affirmation.

Lincoln Schuster to Victor Gollancz, 1936

The fiddles are tuning as it were all over America.

John Butler Yeats, 1912

Unlike other American Lefts, the first Left of the twentieth century was born in a mood of unparalleled optimism. "One's first strong impression," recalled Malcolm Cowley, "is one of the bustle and hopefulness that filled the early years from 1911–1916. . . . Everywhere new institutions were being founded—magazines, clubs, little theatres, art or free-love or single-tax colonies, experimental schools, picture galleries. Everywhere was a sense of comradeship and immense potentialities for change." The new intellectuals' open-air habitat was 73

43 Marcel Duchamp's *Nude Descending a Staircase, No. II,* 1912, one of the Futurist-Cubist paintings that created a furor at the 1913 Armory Show in New York City. The show introduced America to radical new approaches to the visual arts that reflected a corresponding recognition of change and flux in life that animated the Lyrical Left.

Manhattan's Greenwich Village, which Floyd Dell, the chronicler of Village life, called "a moral health resort"; their spiritual home was 23 Fifth Avenue, Mabel Dodge's notorious apartment where anyone and everyone who had a plan to remake the world was welcomed: "Socialists, Trade-Unionists, Anarchists, Suffragists, Poets, Relations, Lawyers, Murderers, 'Old Friends,' Psychoanalysts, I.W.W.'s, Single Taxers, Birth-Controlists, Newspapermen, Artists, Modern-Artists, Clubwomen, Women's-Place-is-in-the-Home Women, Clergymen, and just plain men all met there" to experience "freedom" and exchange "opinions."[1]

EARLY RAPTURES

Dell caught the atmosphere of 1912 when, responding to poetess Edna St. Vincent Millay, he labeled it the "Lyric Year." The period seemed an intellectual Saturnalia in which everything was possible and nothing prohibited, a joyous springtime in which, Mabel Dodge recalled, "barriers went down and people reached each other who had never been in touch before." The mood of America's "New Renaissance" was supremely lyrical, an outpouring of emotions and creative energy that had long been repressed. Responding to the thrilling labor strikes that spread from Lawrence, Massachusetts, to Ludlow, Colorado, the literary Left saw itself as the "music-makers" and "movers and shakers" of a revolutionary culture that aimed to break down the dualism between contemplative life and active life. This poetic passion for releasing the emotions and at the same time unifying thought, feeling, and action gave the first Left its distinctive lyrical style and tone. "Our eyes trained for every seeing," wrote Eastman in 1913, "our ears catching the first murmur of a new experience, we ran after the world in our eagerness, not to learn about it, but to taste the flavor of its being."[2]

Politics and Art

The Lyrical radicals went further than any previous generation in attempting to fuse politics and art. Whereas Emerson and Thoreau looked upon collective action with disdain, the young intellectuals

44 A Greenwich Village (New York City) gathering place of the early 1920's. The inscription reflects the sense of the "Village" as a center of artistic and political ferment of the time.

embraced it with delight. While the Transcendentalists believed politics the realm of opinion and poetry the realm of truth, the new cultural rebellion denied all dichotomies. The Lyrical Left rejected Yeats' contention that poetry and politics, imagination and truth, private vision and public life must inevitably be in eternal opposition. Rather, the appeal of the prewar Left was its all-encompassing "integration of conflicting values . . . : politics, poetry, and science; justice, beauty, and knowledge."[3] The lyrical impulse to synthesize influenced even the sober-minded Walter Lippmann; in *A Preface to Politics* (1913), he sought to humanize government, to elevate it from "routine" procedures and stale formulas so that "the ideals of human feelings" would "place politics among the genuine, creative activities of men." Making man the measure of politics, Lippmann realized, "amounts to saying

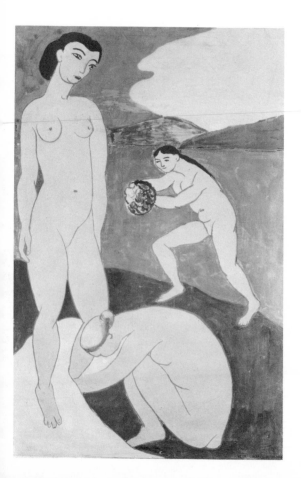

45 Matisse's *Le Luxe*, another painting exhibited at the controversial 1913 Armory Show (see Figure 43).

46 Mabel Dodge, whose home in Greenwich Village became a kind of salon of radical thinkers in the arts and politics.

that the goal of action is in its final analysis aesthetic and not moral—a quality of feeling instead of a conformity to rule."[4]

The young intellectuals cheerfully presided over the death of the "genteel tradition" as they attacked its Victorian standards, polite manners and haute-bourgeois tastes, its Puritan heritage and decorous Brahmin literature, and, above all, its condescending certainty that it had found ultimate truth and absolute value. Forsaking the traditional quest for permanent truth and value, the young intellectuals embarked upon a life that embraced change and flux, a new life that had to be experienced before it could be analyzed. Their odyssey often brought them to Bergson, James, Nietzsche, Freud, and D. H. Lawrence, heralds of the antirationalist power of intuition, desire, will, dream, and instinct. Proclaiming a new ethic of gaiety and sensuality, the Lyrical rebels proudly declared themselves to be reckless and irresponsible. "A feeling of power that translates itself into duty is no fun," advised Mabel Dodge, who believed that "consciousness is more important than heroism or than any given ethical or political point of view, and I believe it more desirable to be ignoble and know it than to be noble and not know it." The "superb modern healthiness" of Dostoevsky, announced Randolph Bourne, is his ability to draw no "dividing line between the normal and the abnormal, or even between the sane and insane." Despite the cult of irresponsibility, many intellectuals who had been brought up in a religious environment carried with them the heritage against which they rebelled. Their passion for social justice, their quest for love and friendship, and their thirst for esthetic experience reflected the internalized values of their Protestant backgrounds. If they rejected the capitalist ethos of striving to make good, many retained the religious ethic of striving to *be* good. In essence, theirs was a Christian culture without Christianity. Even so pagan a libertine as Mabel Dodge could, between taking John Reed as a lover and peyote as an offering, admit in a moment of doubt: "Finally I believed the lack to be in myself when I found myself perpetually unassuaged—and, I thought, only religion will fill me, someday I will find God." But God was dead, and no one knew this better than the generation of 1913.[5]

Although a certain sense of orthodox values and a vague spiritual hunger lingered on, with the collapse of religious beliefs the young intellectuals tried to find meaning and fulfillment in culture, sex, or politics—in many cases all three. Some turned to radical politics for a surrogate religion. For Max Eastman, Marxism would put an end to spiritual anguish: "I need no longer extinguish my dream with my knowledge. I need never again cry out: 'I wish I believed in the Son of God and his second coming.'"[6] Until 1917, when the Bolshevik revolution challenged evolutionary democratic socialism, the Lyrical Left's radicalism drew upon British Fabian and Guild socialism as well as Marxism. The Left's socialism was also an outgrowth of a self-conscious youth culture that, at Harvard and Columbia especially, gave the blasé high school graduate the option of radical activism or *Kulturpessimismus*. Students debated socialism in classrooms, fraternities, and at the meetings of the Intercollegiate Socialist Society, where wealthy young scions from the Ivy League listened to Jack London, the golden-boy dropout who was becoming America's first millionaire novelist, lecture on the beauties of the social revolution.

Diversity of Appeal

Socialism appealed to intellectuals for various reasons. Eastman saw socialism both as a science and as an esthetic liberation that would bring forth a life of creative leisure. The whimsical playboy John Reed hoped that struggling for socialism would overcome the *mauvais foi* that plagued him and other middle-class intellectuals: "My happiness is built on the misery of others . . . that fact poisons me, disturbs my serenity, and makes me write propaganda when I would rather play."[7] Lippmann, precocious social philosopher and leading figure in the Harvard Socialist Club, considered socialism as the only alternative to the corruption of Tammany Hall and the power of big business. Yet it is significant that Lippmann, one of the first American intellectuals to see the relevance to politics of the new irrationalist psychology, was also one of the first of the Lyrical Left to have reservations about socialism. Convinced that any political movement must be built upon a realistic theory of human nature, Lippmann found socialism wanting in two respects: its idolization of the masses ignored the widespread visceral need for heroic leaders, and its faith in the inevitable polarization of classes scarcely took into account the complexity of America's multiclass structure. At the same time, Lippmann rejected the argument of Walling's *Progressivism and After,* that the transition to socialism would be gradual, proceeding from the state capitalism of the industrialists to the progressive reforms of the middle class. Dismissing Walling's reasoning as an expression of the "American Dream," Lippmann believed that socialism could be achieved, if at all, only by organized pressure from the lower classes. That conviction attracted him to the IWW. Although the Wobblies scorned political activity, ignored the probability that the state would not disappear after capitalism, and seemed not to realize that workers' syndicates could exploit consumers as much as industrialists, Lippmann still believed the IWW possessed tremendous potential because, unlike all other radical movements, "It has practiced actual solidarity." Lippmann refrained from glorifying the IWW, which he regarded as capable of only "insurrection," but he could agree with Eastman that it was "the only genuinely *proletarian* or revolutionary organization that ever existed in America."[8]

The New Review and *The Masses*

The first twentieth-century American Left advertised itself in two different publications, *The New Review* and *The Masses.* The former reflected its sober mind, the latter its soaring spirit. In *The New Review* the Left debated the basic issues facing socialism, carried symposia on the feminist movement, and explored the relatively new field of Negro history. But this sophisticated theoretical journal was overshadowed by *The Masses*, perhaps the heartiest journal in the history of American radicalism. Free of doctrinal strain, *The Masses* gave radicalism a well-needed lift of laughter. Satirical but not cynical, audacious but not self-righteous, it was animated by eight passions: "fun, truth, beauty, realism, freedom, peace, feminism, revolution."[9] Its masthead promised *The Masses* would please no one and delight everyone:

A REVOLUTIONARY AND NOT A REFORM MAGAZINE: A MAGAZINE WITH A SENSE OF HUMOR AND NO RESPECT FOR THE RESPECTABLE: FRANK, ARROGANT, IMPERTINENT, SEARCHING FOR THE TRUE CAUSES: A MAGAZINE DIRECTED AGAINST RIGIDITY AND DOGMA WHEREVER IT IS FOUND: PRINTING WHAT IS TOO NAKED OR TRUE FOR A MONEY-MAKING PRESS: A MAGAZINE WHOSE FINAL POLICY IS TO DO AS IT PLEASES AND CONCILIATE NOBODY, NOT EVEN ITS READERS.

Edited by Eastman with the help of Dell and Reed, *The Masses* featured young poets and novelists, reputable journalists, and talented artists and cartoonists who depicted the foibles of the rich and the frustrations of the poor. The breezy combination of bohemianism and radicalism was too much for the stolid labor Left and the old-time socialists like W. J. Ghent, who complained of *The Masses:* "It is peculiarly the product of the restless metropolitan coteries who devote themselves to the cult of Something Else: who are ever seeking the bubble Novelty even at the door of Bedlam."[10] One wit wondered how *The Masses* ever expected to reach the masses:

> They draw nude women for the *Masses*
> Thick, fat, ungainly lasses —
> How does that help the working classes?[11]

Socialist attacks failed to dampen the confident bravado of the Lyrical Left, which did its best to help the lower classes by raising funds for striking coal and textile workers, by publicizing the plight of immigrants and blacks, and by speaking truth to power. What would undermine its optimism was the subsequent challenge of historic events.

47 A John Sloan cartoon from *The Masses,* entitled "She Got the Point," comments on the rising feminist awareness of the time. The woman in the foreground says to her companion: "You'd better be good Jim, or I'll join 'em." W.S.P. (on the banner) stands for Women's Suffrage Party.

CHALLENGES AND CONFLICT

War and the State

The first challenge to the ideals of the Left came with the outbreak of the First World War in August 1914. From the establishment of the First International in 1864 to Trotsky's attempt to start a Fourth International in 1939, the ideal of an international working-class community loomed as the great hope of the Left. In the years before the war, when the ideal seemed close to realization, American radicals assumed that European workers had achieved the political strength and maturity to oppose war and declare their solidarity with the Second International. When war came, however, most socialist parliamentarians approved military budgets in their respective governments, while workers responded to the call of nationalism. Radicals had earlier been able to mount antiwar demonstrations, but once war was declared there were

81

no mass protests, no general strikes, no worldwide labor boycotts. The proletariat marched off to battle with the rest of the human race.

In December 1914, the American SP issued a manifesto condemning the war, announcing its neutrality, and declaring it the "supreme duty" of socialists to rededicate themselves to the "imperishable principles of international socialism." The manifesto created bitter inner-party debate. To moderates like Hillquit and Spargo the crisis of European socialism made it clear that workers ultimately placed their country before their class and that, thus, the concept of proletarian internationalism was a "frail wand." The more militant Marxists, like Louis Fraina and Louis Boudin, however, now began to trace the origins of the war to imperialism, an exercise that enabled them to sustain some faith in the misguided masses and to suggest that a new International, purged of all prowar elements, could be organized. The majority of socialist intellectuals and labor leaders changed their positions for various reasons. Some shifted to intervention because of a simple concern for national security; others feared that a Prussianized, imperialistic Germany presented a threat to democracy and the Left; still others believed that the war might hasten the coming of socialism as the government

48 Writer Upton Sinclair, one of many celebrated intellectuals who left the Socialist Party during the controversy over its stand on America's entry into the war in 1917.

49 A female Secret Service operative infiltrates the alleged women's branch of the IWW in a scene from a propaganda film made in 1918.

nationalized industry. For three years the Left continued to debate the nature and consequences of the war. By April 1917, when President Wilson went before Congress to ask for a declaration of war, most leading socialist writers had already advocated America's intervention. Despite the defection of intellectual luminaries like Walling, London, Simons, and Upton Sinclair, the SP convention issued another antiwar resolution the day after Wilson's address to Congress. The resolution, approved by three-fourths of the delegates, had the support of political leaders like Debs, Hillquit, and Berger. The SP's courageous action proved to be a short-run triumph and a long-run disaster. Shortly afterwards the SP increased its membership by more than 12,000, and in various municipal elections in June socialist candidates gained new support from antiwar voters. But ultimately the SP suffered a psychic wound as members began to accuse one another of class betrayal or national treason. The prowar socialist Charles E. Russell thought his former comrades "should be driven out of the country," and the millionaire socialist J. G. Phelps Stokes suggested they be "shot at once without an hour's delay."[12]

Though the government did not go that far, it went far enough. In June 1917, Congress passed the Espionage Act (supplemented in 1918 by a Sedition Act), that forbade all obstruction of the war effort. Immediately the U.S. Post Office denied mailing privileges to socialist publications, and while editors tried vainly to fight their case in court, the government moved against the SP itself. Before the war was over almost every major SP official had been indicted for antiwar activity. Enraged mobs had also cracked down on radical dissent everywhere. Throughout the country IWW headquarters were raided. In Oklahoma, Wobblies were rounded up and tarred and feathered; in Arizona they were packed into cattle cars and abandoned in the desert; and in Montana, Frank Little, a crippled IWW leader, was kidnapped and hanged from a railway trestle. The repression bore down heavily on antiwar liberals as well. At Columbia University three professors were fired for having criticized American intervention, whereupon the eminent historian Charles Beard resigned in protest. Watching this affair, Columbia graduate Randolph Bourne visited one of the dismissed professors, his friend Harold C. Dana.

> "And now that you have been expelled, Harry, will you make the scandal?"
> "Certainly not," Dr. Dana said. "I've given my word as a gentleman."
> "That's the trouble," Bourne replied with a wide grin. "You look upon all this as a gentlemen's quarrel. You lack Homeric anger."[13]

Gentlemen scholars were not the only ones who disappointed the Lyrical Left. Everywhere the intellectual community seemed to be capitulating. Isadora Duncan, who once symbolized the liberating joys of the body, was now performing patriotic dances in the Metropolitan Opera House. Former *Masses* contributors had gone to work for the Committee on Public Information, Wilson's official propaganda agency; honored intellectuals like Veblen, Dewey, and the former socialist Lippmann had also come out strongly in support of America's entry into the war.

The Lyrical Left, always an uneasy alliance of disparate radicals with different causes, was now hopelessly divided by the war. Randolph Bourne leveled the most devastating attack on the prowar intellectuals. Bourne, who had once studied under Dewey, could not accept his argument that the conscientious objector should "attach his conscience and intelligence to forces moving in another direction" in order to assure that the war be elevated toward democratic ends. "War," Bourne pointed out, "determines its own end—victory, and government crushes out automatically all forces that deflect, or threaten to deflect, energy from the path of organization to that end." Similarly Eastman could not accept Walling's argument that intellectuals must "adjust themselves to events." A war based upon "blind tribal instincts," Eastman pointed out, rendered events beyond rational control. Like Bourne, Eastman saw "no connection with its causes or the conscious purposes of those who fight. . . . It is a war of national invasion and defense—nationalism, the most banal of stupid idol-worships." John Reed also warned of the "judicial tyranny, bureaucratic suppression, and industrial barbarism,

50 Wobblies interned by the government in 1917 because of their antiwar views.

which followed inevitably the first careless rapture of militarism." What remained of the Lyrical Left, then, rejected both the assumption, held by some socialists, that a war economy offered the possibility of industrial collectivism and the hope, held by many Liberals, that the war could bring about worldwide democracy. "For once the babes and sucklings seem to have been wiser than the children of light," observed Bourne.[14]

The behavior of prowar writers like Walling and Lippmann also revived the Marxist distrust of a young "intellectual proletariat." The New Intellectuals that had earlier been hailed as a potential revolutionary vanguard now appeared to be "a corrupt and corrupting influence [whose] petty bourgeois souls scent the flesh pots of Imperialism. . . . In every imperialistic country it is precisely these 'workers of the brain' who manufacture and carry into the ranks of the workers the ideology and the enthusiasm of Imperialism."[15] Although the Lyrical Left's idealism was severely damaged by the defection of the intellectuals, the

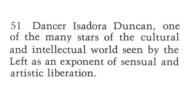

51 Dancer Isadora Duncan, one of the many stars of the cultural and intellectual world seen by the Left as an exponent of sensual and artistic liberation.

52 From left, Crystal Eastman, Art Young, Max Eastman, Morris Hillquit, Merrill Rogers, Jr., and Floyd Dell at the time of their indictment under the Sedition Act of 1918 for opposing America's entry into the First World War.

real deathblow came from the response of the masses to the war. The popular upsurge of nationalism was a source of repression that the Left had not fully anticipated. Eastman and Bourne pondered the social and psychological meaning of war and nationalism in two significant essays: "The Religion of Patriotism," that Eastman wrote in 1916, and "The State," that Bourne started in 1917 but did not finish before his untimely death the following year. Both Eastman and Bourne believed that the war had laid bare the "gregarious instinct" and "herd impulse" of the human animal, and by transforming man's aggressive drives into illusions of power and idealism had brought about a nationalistic solidarity that strangled critical intelligence. "There is nothing more copiously able to bind into its bosom the multiple threads of human impulse, and establish that fixed and absolute glorious tyranny among our purposes, than military patriotism," wrote Eastman. "The nation in

87

war-time," observed Bourne, "attains a uniformity of feeling, a hierarchy of values culminating at the undisputed apex of the State ideal. . . . The individual as a social being in war seems to have achieved almost his apotheosis." More than culture or class conflict, war was the real catalyst that moved the masses to idealistic acts of self-sacrifice and delusions of "organic" wholeness. In despair, Bourne penned an epigram for a whole generation when he shrewdly commented: "War is the health of the State."[16]

Bolshevism: The Triumph

Four thousand miles away an obscure Russian exile, Vladimir Ilich Lenin, reached the opposite conclusion. In his anarcho-syndicalist *State and Revolution* (1917) Lenin seemed to show that war was the sickness of the state and the health of revolution. In the eyes of the American Left, Lenin would soon emerge as the prophet who proved his theory of power.

In February 1917, the Russian tsarist government collapsed with the dull thud of an historic anachronism; in October the bolsheviks swept into power. The American Left reacted enthusiastically to the first event and ecstatically to the second. Although the triumph of Lenin defied the "laws" of Marxism, it answered the needs of American radicals. The last place a proletarian revolution was expected to occur was in Russia, a backward country that lacked the industrial base to make the transition to socialism. Moreover, the revolution appeared to have been "made" by the determined imagination and will of a small minority of 12,000 party leaders and intellectuals. It seemed that in Russia the radical intelligentsia had found at last a way to socialism that bypassed the long, arduous route of reform. If Russian intellectuals could create a revolution in an agricultural country, what could stop American intellectuals from doing the same in an industrialized society? To America's Left, dejected and rendered powerless by the war, Lenin's stunning achievement was Marx's second coming.

Not surprisingly, the American Left interpreted the revolution in its own disparate ideological images and every faction identified with the bolsheviks. Eastman believed that even the February Revolution created in one blow a "Syndicalist-Socialist Russia." When the bolsheviks triumphed over the Provisional Government, the DeLeonists claimed that the wisdom of revolutionary industrial unionism had been proven. Reed's eyewitness account, *Ten Days That Shook the World,* was later smuggled to the Wobbly prisoners in Leavenworth Penitentiary, and the old Wobbly official Harold Varney announced that "Bolshevism was but the Russian name for IWW." Even reformist socialists who had denounced the doctrine of violence came to the defense of the violent bolsheviks. James Oneal ridiculed those who protested that "there has been violence in Russia. Some violence in a revolution! Just imagine! Do they think a revolution is a pink tea party?" Moderate leaders like Hillquit defended the "dictatorship of the proletariat" as democratic; and Debs, the most gentle radical of all, proclaimed: "From the crown of

53 In a cartoon from *The Masses,* one bloated plutocrat: "But we can't send 'em all off to the war to be killed. We've got to have 'em around to keep wages down." And the reply: "M-m, and if they stay here they may join the IWW and raise hell."

my head to the soles of my feet I am a Bolshevik, and proud of it." Emma Goldman and Alexander Berkman immediately sailed off to Russia to witness what they assumed would be the glorious birth of anarchism, and Lincoln Steffens returned from Russia to tell Americans, "I have been over into the future, and it works."[17]

One cannot overemphasize the utopian, democratic image that surrounded bolshevism in its first months in power. The image of a "peoples' democracy" and a "commune state" enraptured the entire spectrum of the American Left: anarchists, syndicalists, revolutionary socialists, democratic socialists, and even a number of pacifists, social reformers, and liberal intellectuals. One by one most of these elements grew disenchanted with bolshevism, and within a few years its remaining American admirers dwindled to a small circle of comrades whose infatuation with Soviet power bore little resemblance to the original ideals of the American Left. Two developments account for the change of attitudes toward Russia: the centralization of the American communist parties, and the Stalinization of international communism.

When the bolsheviks seized power, American radicals wanted to prove that they too were revolutionaries and not timid "mensheviks" or discredited reformers. This impulse led native radicals to look to the Russian-language Federation in the SP as the organic tie to bolshevism. The Russian Federation was composed of recent Slavic immigrants who knew almost nothing about bolshevism, but the Russian-Americans encouraged the illusion that only they could speak for Lenin and Trotsky. The left wing began to champion the Russian Federation, which, together with the Polish, Hungarian, Ukrainian, Lithuanian, Lettish, and Dutch federations, comprised a majority in the SP. The spokesman for the left wing was Louis Fraina. A brilliant young Marxist and one of the founding fathers of American communism, Fraina had developed a new theory of "mass action" in *Revolutionary Socialism* (1918). In February 1919, militants issued Fraina's "Left-Wing Manifesto," which condemned the right wing for its tepid "sausage socialism" and, in the spirit of Russian bolshevism, called upon Americans to organize workers' councils as a means of taking power and establishing a proletarian dictatorship in the United States. The following month the Third International was born in Moscow. In order to disassociate themselves

54   In its art as in its poetry, the Lyrical Left was moved to rapture by the example
of Lenin's achievement.

from the social democrats, the bolsheviks revived Marx's use of the term
"communism." The new Communist International (soon condensed to
"Comintern") ordered every socialist party in the world to split from its
right-wing factions. A fierce struggle now ensued for control of American socialism. A national referendum indicated that the majority of
socialists desired to join the Third International, and another referendum for the election of a new National Executive Committee gave a
decisive majority to the left wing. But the right wing simply dismissed
the vote and began to suspend the seven left-wing, foreign-language   91

federations. Within six months the SP lost two-thirds of its membership, declining from 109,589 to 39,750. Disgusted, left-wing leaders bolted and formed a separate communist organization, which immediately broke into two factions, the Communist Party and the Communist Labor Party. The larger CP was made up of the foreign-language federations and headed by Fraina and Charles Ruthenberg; the smaller CLP of native American radicals was led by Reed and Benjamin Gitlow. Although the CP and CLP fought incessantly over organizational questions and over the "correct" interpretation of Marxist-Leninism, both groups espoused the revolutionary imperative of "mass action."[18]

In the year 1919, which Dos Passos likened to "the springtime of revolution," things did seem ripe for a radical solution. Labor unrest had gripped the country as longshoremen, printers, switchmen, tailors, garment workers, telephone personnel, streetcar conductors, and garbage collectors walked off their jobs. Outside the numerous plants of United States Steel some 367,000 workers took turns on the picket line for a period of four months; in Seattle a city-wide strike was called; and in Boston salary-gouged policemen did not report for work, whereupon scores of college students, answering Governor Coolidge's call to God and country, helped maintain law and order. Yet while one of the greatest strike waves in American history was taking place, communists remained on the sidelines, scorning the reforms demanded by workers and condemning trade unionism. The Bolshevik revolution taught American communists to hold out for nothing less than revolution. But as they awaited the "inevitable" revolution, the predictable reaction set in. Wartime espionage and sedition laws were now used against communists and anarchists as Attorney General Palmer directed unannounced raids against their homes and headquarters. During the Red Scare of 1919 and the early 1920's the membership of both communist parties declined from over 60,000 to under 10,000. The remaining dedicated communists decided to go underground. Life in secret cell meetings increased their revolutionary fervor. Now American communists could regard themselves as real bolsheviks, hounded by the police just as Lenin and Trotsky had been hounded by the Tsar's Ochrana. Repression in America, as in Tsarist Russia, was merely further proof that revolution was just around the corner.

55 Ben Shahn's *The Passion of Sacco and Vanzetti* commemorates the execution of the two anarchists accused of murder and robbery. The case was a *cause célèbre* of what little remained of the prewar Left in the 1920's.

56   Leftists being taken into custody during one of the raids directed by United States Attorney General Palmer in the 1920's.

Bolshevism: The Disenchantment

By the time the Red Scare had passed and the communists surfaced in late 1921, the international situation had begun to change. Even though American communists could not give up their revolutionary illusions, Lenin was shrewd enough to realize that while it still might be inevitable, revolution was no longer imminent. In *"Left-Wing" Communism: An Infantile Disorder* (1920), Lenin lashed out at the revolutionary impatience of the ultra-Left communists in the West. The two American parties, the CP and the CLP, had already been ordered by the Comintern to bury their differences and unite into one organization. American communists willingly accepted this directive from Moscow. But Lenin's tactical shift to the right came as a shock to many members. For communists were now told to establish a legitimate party, engage in electoral activity, and later to form "united fronts" with other progressive groups. Even more stunning, they were ordered to work within rather than against unions, not to destroy the AFL but to infiltrate it. This was the most painful irony of all. Lenin, the uncompromising revolutionary, was now ordering American radicals to practice what they had denounced the SP for engaging in since the turn of the century —political activity and trade unionism. These decisions bewildered left-wing leaders like Haywood and Fraina, who were to become increasingly disenchanted with the Moscow-dominated CP. But others stayed in the CP and subordinated themselves to the Comintern.

The remaining history of the CP during the twenties is a grotesque story of inner-party struggle, ego rivalry, and character assassination. *The Communist, Workers Monthly,* and *Revolutionary Age* occasionally featured high-level theoretical discussions. The controversy over "American exceptionalism"—can America's historical and economic development be understood solely in Marxist terms; and, if not, must America find its own way to the goals of Marx?—laid the groundwork for a half century of subsequent debate among American radical intellectuals. Yet what is significant about the factional debates of the 1920's is the manner in which they were resolved. In almost every instance the disputes were settled, despite the majority will of the American CP, either by a cablegram from the Comintern or by a trip to Moscow. This deference made the American CP an instrument that Joseph Stalin, the new dictator of the Soviet Union, gladly exploited to further Russia's interests. "Can anyone in his right mind," the Trotskyist Max Schactman would later lament, "imagine leaders of socialism like Lenin, Trotsky, Plekhanov, . . . Debs, DeLeon, Haywood . . . racing back and forth between their countries and the seat of the Second International, appealing to its Executive to make the decision on what policy their parties should be commanded to adopt?"[19] The generation of 1913 could not have imagined such a spectacle. The Stalinization of the American Left was the end of radical innocence.

During the 1920's communism had few admirers among those who had been the prewar intellectual rebels. Lenin's *State and Revolution* was compatible with the anarcho-syndicalist visions of *The Masses* circle; but his *"Left-Wing" Communism* could hardly inspire those who once believed that "infantile disorder" was part of revolutionary adventure. Older socialists like Hillquit and liberals like Steffens continued to defend the Soviet Union against its conservative critics in America. But those closer to the spirit of the prewar rebellion found nothing to defend. Emma Goldman, the anarchist heroine of the Lyr-

57 Anarchist and feminist Emma Goldman, one of the first to admire and one of the first to be disillusioned by the Soviet Union.

ical Left, watched in horror as Lenin crushed the Russian anarchists in the Kronstadt uprising in 1921, and embattled Wobblies soon gave up hope that Russian workers would have their own independent unions under bolshevism or that American workers would have their own voice in the CP. Ultimately communism became a repudiation of two basic ideals that had inspired the Lyrical Left: the autonomy of the intellectual and the self-liberation of the working class. Under Stalin political "truth" became the test of culture and the intellectual was forced to defend, not the unorganized American workers, but the tightly organized Communist Party.

THE ODYSSEYS OF REED AND EASTMAN
TWO PATTERNS OF DISILLUSIONMENT

Typical of the disillusionment of what remained of the Lyrical Left were the reactions of John Reed and Max Eastman.

Reed

John Silas Reed's transformation from a lonely, insecure, wealthy student to a dedicated revolutionary who died in Russia of malnutrition and typhus is an experience in some ways unique, in some typical of the Left intellectual of the period. Unlike most early American communists, Reed was neither an immigrant, a city-bred easterner, a self-educated worker-intellectual, nor a stern Marxist ideologue. A robust, pleasure-loving youth who would become an acquaintance of Lenin and Trotsky, an important American figure in the early Comintern, a patron saint of the American Communist Party, and a hero buried near the Kremlin wall along with the fallen heroes of 1917, Reed was as American as breakfast cereal.

Born and raised in an elegant mansion in Portland, Oregon, Reed attended prep school and then Harvard, where his greatest thrill was becoming the star cheerleader and enjoying "the blissful sensation of swaying two thousand voices in great crashing choruses during the football games." In college he was indifferent to politics and regarded his courses as insipid exercises one had to endure while gaining a place in the prestigious social clubs. When Lincoln Steffens came to interview him about a position in journalism, Reed told his idol of his ambitions: "To make a million dollars . . . to get married . . . to write my name in letters of fire against the sky." Reed's ambition for fame and fortune sprang from a deeper romantic desire, a restless, Byronic temperament that enabled him to become, without much ideological reflection, the poet-playboy of the Lyrical Left. Reed inherited his father's sympathy for the underdog, and his passionate commitment to verse suggests that his radicalism also grew out of an esthetic temperament, a Faustian hunger for the fullness of life. He was easily moved by the drama of history and the majesty of great men and great deeds. "History was my passion, kings strutting about and armored ranks of men," he recalled. Later, in Venice with Mabel Dodge, he repeated to her the beauties of history. "The things *men* have done! But I wish that *I* could have been there at the *doing* of it, or that they were doing it now."[20]

When Reed moved to Greenwich Village, he instantly fell in love with the bohemian culture, New York's "wild ungovernable youth" whose "monuments uncouth" produced in him "a fierce joy of creation." Here Reed also fell in love with Mabel Dodge. "His olive green eyes glowed softly," sighed Dodge, "his high forehead was like a baby's with light brown curls rolling away from it and two spots of shining light on his temples, making him lovable. His chin was the best . . . the real poet's jawbone . . . eyebrows always lifted . . . generally breathless!"[21] During the joyous years before the war Reed wrote winsome

97

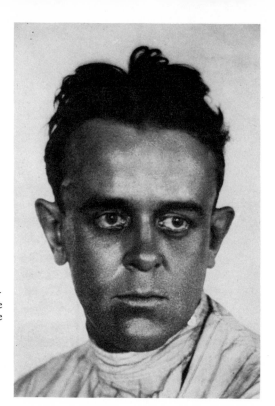

58 John Reed, poet-journalist and revolutionary, one of the romantic heroes of the Lyrical Left.

verse, participated in the Paterson, New Jersey, garment workers' strike (during which he was jailed and organized the subsequently famous Paterson strike pageant), tried peyote ("these nauseatingly bitter buttons"), lived with various Village girls, and, on a trip to Paris, showed Mabel Dodge "what a honeymoon should be." But Reed soon became absorbed by the course of world events, and in 1913 he abandoned "man-eating Mabel" to see and write about war and revolution. His career from this point on reads like a Hemingway postscript to *Huckleberry Finn*. With an army of *companeros* he rode through Mexico to write about the exploits of the Robin Hood revolutionary Pancho Villa; a year later, when war broke out in Europe, he was off to France and then to the dreary eastern front; and after returning to the United States in 1917, he again rushed off to Russia as soon as he heard that the Romanov dynasty had crumbled.[22]

Reed arrived in Russia two months before the bolsheviks came to power. Immediately he visited the liberal democrats' Duma, made his way into the bolshevik headquarters and interviewed its leaders, then addressed bewildered Russian workers in English, sped around Petrograd in a truck passing out Russian-language leaflets that he could not read, and participated in the storming of the Winter Palace, smuggling out a jewel-handled sword for a souvenir. Reed's sympathy for the downtrodden and his attraction to bold, dynamic leaders moved him to side with the bolsheviks. As he watched them seizing power he collected every item he could find—leaflets, newspapers, reports, resolutions, interviews, press clippings, peeled-off posters—to use in writing his vivid account of the greatest social cataclysm in modern history, *Ten Days That Shook the World.* Reed came back to the United States a confirmed bolshevik, but just how long he remained so is a matter of controversy. In 1919 he returned to Russia to seek a solution to the factionalism that had split the two American communist parties. He arrived suffering from scurvy and malnutrition after two months of hunger and filth in a Finnish jail. Already distraught because of his illness, he became demoralized when he saw the suffering of the Russian people. The final blow was his treatment by Zinoviev and Radek, the Comintern's two leading officials. Reed had been at odds with the Comintern since it had announced its new trade-union line. To Reed the Bolshevik revolution had been like the fulfillment of a Wobbly dream, an egalitarian uprising that put an end to all authority. Now new authorities were ordering American radicals to forsake the IWW and join the AFL. When officials tried to prevent Reed from presenting his case before the Second Congress of the Comintern, he resigned in disgust from its Executive Committee. No doubt Reed was appalled by the high-handed methods of the Comintern, but whether he had made a complete break with communism before his death is another question.

In an authoritative analysis, "The Mystery of John Reed," Theodore Draper concluded that there was no evidence of a "final accounting" and "definitive break" with communism. "But if disillusionment is understood intellectually and emotionally, Reed was probably as disillusioned as it was possible to be and still remain in the movement. His disillusionment was cumulative, and it was heading toward a break on both sides if he had persisted on his course." Had Reed lived it is most likely that he would have resigned from the CP if the CP did not expel him first. Yet it is doubtful that Reed would have become a renegade from radicalism, as did much of the Old Left of the 1930's. As Draper puts it: "Disillusionment there was, deeply implanted, but . . . John Reed had probably paid for his faith too dearly to give it up without another struggle."[23] This struggle might have brought him to side with Trotsky (a hero of *Ten Days That Shook the World*), the course taken by the other remaining spirit of the Lyrical Left, Max Eastman.

Eastman

Like Reed, Eastman came from a Protestant, upper-middle-class background, and he too experienced all the tensions that parental dependency, sexual awareness, and religious doubt could produce in a sensitive adolescent. Unlike Reed, with his youthful romantic egotism, Eastman expressed a combination of paganism and piety. His "heroic" mother and "sainted" father were both Congregational ministers, and their "Christian ideal," he later recalled, "demands that life itself, as we live it, be transcended and superseded and changed. It is a utopian ideal, and ethically, at least, revolutionary."[24] This evangelical environment was the source of Eastman's social radicalism and also his

59 Big Bill Haywood of the IWW pays his respects at the grave of John Reed in Moscow.

moral conservatism, which made him uncomfortable with the flaunting libertinism of some of his comrades. Eastman was also more learned than the younger Reed and the other *Masses* writers. Something of a Renaissance radical, he would write over twenty books dealing with art, science, poetry, philosophy, humor, journalism, esthetics, anthropology, religion, Marxism, German politics, and Freudian psychology, as well as five volumes of verse, a novel, two volumes of brilliant biographical portraits, and a study of the young Trotsky. After mastering Russian in a little more than a year, he translated the works of Pushkin and Trotsky, edited Marx's momentous *Das Kapital,* and clipped together a film documentary on the Russian Revolution.

Tall, lean, tanned, and strikingly handsome with his blond wavy hair and deep, pensive eyes, Eastman was the best-known literary radical of his generation. "He looked Beauty and spoke Justice," exclaimed a close friend.[25] Eastman's life before the war was one continual round of cultural and political activities. He brought the Wobblies' struggle to public attention, championed the radical feminists, and, together with his sister Crystal, organized the American Union Against Militarism. Before the bolsheviks came to power none of *The Masses* group had heard of Lenin, and even afterwards so little was known of him in the United States that his name was frequently misspelled. But Eastman immediately sensed the man's greatness. To Eastman, Lenin was a philosopher-king and a social engineer whose language "was that of astute, flexible, undoctrinaire, unbigoted, supremely purposive, and, I judged, experimental intelligence." Eastman came to believe that Marxism's "dialectical reason" implied a practical mode of thought unencumbered by the constricting demands of abstract theory, and he would later quote Lenin as saying, "Flexibility of conception, flexibility to the point of the identity of opposite—that is the essence of the dialectic." All this was seductive. No doubt Lenin was a practical genius who acted pragmatically and realistically, but Eastman assumed that Marxism itself represented an open-ended, pragmatic philosophy. "To me the procedure was experimental, and the ideas were subject to correction." At bottom, Marxism appealed to Eastman's two contradictory impulses—his idealism and his realism, his yearning for the imaginative world of the possible beyond the actual, and his dispassionate

101

scientific respect for the actual world of facts and experience. "It was this clash of impetuosities, the thirst of extreme ideals and the argumentative clinging to facts, which led me to seize so joyfully upon Marx's idea of progress through class struggle." As a philosophical proposition, Marxism seemed the resolution of the eternal dualism of facts and values, science and esthetics, reality and desire. Marxism also appeared to have resolved one of the greatest problems in social theory: how to attain a perfect society with imperfect human beings. Eastman recalled Mark Twain's answer when the novelist was asked what he thought about socialism: "I can't even hope for it. I know too much about human nature." Marxism offered a solution to Twain's and Eastman's dilemma. While acknowledging the limitations of historic man, it enabled contemporary man "to line up fiercely with the ideal against the real." As a dialectical philosophy that negated all dualisms, Marxism resolved all contradictions.

> This man Marx seemed to offer a scheme for attaining the ideal based on the very facts which make it otherwise unattainable. Instead of trying to change human nature, I said to myself, he takes human nature as it is, and with that as a driving force tries to change the conditions that make it work badly. Far from glorying in a new "conversion," I was loath even to call my new-found equilibrium socialism. I called it "hard-headed idealism."[26]

Eastman would later re-examine his "Americanization of Marxism." Meanwhile he enthusiastically supported the left-wing socialists who wanted to break with the SP, and his new paper, *The Liberator* (successor to the government-suppressed *Masses*), endorsed the Comintern. But as with Reed, Eastman's ardor began to cool when he visited Russia in 1922 "to find out whether what I have been saying is true." At first he was impressed by the Red Army and by the energy and health of the Russian people. Bolshevik leaders gratefully received him as a trusted ally, and Trotsky befriended him as an intellectual comrade. But while Eastman toured the countryside and studied Russian in the Marx-Engels Institute Library, Stalin began to launch the campaign against Trotsky. Even though Eastman attended the 1923 Party Congress he was "unaware of the beastlike struggle for power that was in progress behind the scenes of this high-minded discussion." Then the *danse macabre*

THE   MARCH 1918   15 CENTS

LIBERATOR

MAX EASTMAN, Editor

John Reed's
Story of the
Bolsheviki
Revolution

60   An issue of *The Liberator* when it was under the editorship of Max Eastman.

unfolded with Lenin's death in January 1924. As the party hacks or *"apparatchiks "* began their move against the anti-Stalin opposition, Trotsky advised Eastman to leave the country with documents that would expose Russia's internal struggle for power. Those documents included a section of Lenin's last "Testament," in which the Premier, dictating on his deathbed, called for Stalin's removal from the post of General Secretary. Eastman published them in 1925 in *Since Lenin Died*, and he defended Trotsky as a "genius" whose "superior moral and intellectual revolutionary greatness" made him Lenin's logical successor. Trotsky's failure to act upon those revelations and the defeat of the opposition in Russia made the Stalinization of American communism a certainty.[27]

Unlike Reed, Eastman had not been troubled by Lenin's shift to the right on the trade union issue, which could be regarded as evidence of Lenin's ideological flexibility. Actually it was Trotsky, Eastman's hero, who turned out to be the hesitating Hamlet, the "unarmed prophet" who failed to act pragmatically and decisively. But the defeat of the anti-Stalinist opposition was not the only cause of Eastman's disillusionment. He had always been uneasy because Russian bolsheviks relied upon Marxism as a body of "sacred scripture" instead of a "working hypothesis." He now began to explore the philosophical foundations of Marxism by studying its most esoteric premise: "dialectical materialism." In *Marx and Lenin: The Science of Revolution* (1927), and in several other essays, running debates, and books published subsequently, Eastman posed two simple but embarrassing epistemological questions: how did Marx come to know what he knew, and how do we know that it is true?

According to Eastman, Marx did not arrive at his understanding of the meaning and direction of history from an objective, scientific study of present and past societies. Instead, Marx's conviction that society moves, through determined stages, toward an inevitable goal derived from the philosophy of Hegel. The dialectical philosophy of Hegel postulated an "inner logic" in history, a universal law of motion that revolved around the principle of contradiction and reconciliation. Marx transferred this principle of change through conflict and resolution from the realm of abstract ideas to the world of concrete social reality. Thus, he assumed that capitalism harbored the "seeds of its own destruction," that it produced its own "contradiction" when it created an industrial proletariat, which in turn would revolt against capitalism and usher in the final resolution, the "end of pre-history"—socialism. To Eastman, this system of historical reasoning seemed like a form of "animistic thinking." Just as primitive man attributed human values and ideals to trees and other natural objects, Marx attributed to the natural processes of history the unfolding of human ideals. Marx accepted Hegel, Eastman argued, in much the same way as nonscientific man accepts "religion"—as a means of reconciling himself to a universe in which he feels alienated. Marx believed in the coming of revolution because his belief enabled him to overcome his estrangement from a world without justice, meaning, or value. Thus he read into history his own purposes and desires, telling it, not like it was, but as he wished it to be. In short, Hegelianism enabled Marx to identify the desirable with the inevitable—an identification Eastman rejected as a Freudian expression of the "rationalization of wish." The crux of Eastman's critique of dialectical materialism was to show that belief in the inevitability of communism was not a scientific proposition. That capitalism morally "ought" to collapse was no basis for predicting that it would.[28]

The original spirits of the first Left of the twentieth century, John Reed and Max Eastman offered no inspiring legacy to future generations of the American Left. In the thirties, Reed, the "lost revolutionary," would be rediscovered by a younger generation as a symbol of bohemian radicalism while communists manipulated his legend to suit the party line. Eastman, a pariah to the communists, would gain the respect of a few anti-Stalinist Left intellectuals of the late thirties for his support of Trotsky and his critiques of dialectical philosophy[29]—and even in the early phase of the New Left, the Berkeley activist Mario Savio could say: "A lot of Hegel got mixed in with Marx's notion of history. Max Eastman pointed this out. The dialectic was a way in which Marx made the course of history coincide with his own unconscious desires."[30] But by and large the Old Left of the 1930's and the New Left of the 1960's knew little or nothing of the experiences of the founding generation of the American Left. Much of the Old Left would willingly accept the Comintern domination that Reed so vigorously resisted, and the New Left would later, with the help of Herbert Marcuse, celebrate the very Hegelianism in Marx which Eastman so deftly disclosed. Perhaps each generation must re-enact the ceremony of innocence; each must repudiate the past even while repeating it.

Notes

[1] Malcolm Cowley, quoted in William E. Leuchtenburg, *The Perils of Prosperity, 1914–1932* (Chicago: Univ. of Chicago Press, 1958), p. 140; Floyd Dell, *Homecoming*, pp. 356–59; Mabel Dodge Luhan, *Intimate Memoirs*, Vol. III, *Movers and Shakers* (New York: Kraus, 1936), pp. 39, 83.

[2] Max Eastman, *Enjoyment of Poetry* (New York: Scribner, 1913), pp. 10–11; see also Van Wyck Brooks, *America's Coming-of-Age* (New York: Dutton, 1915).

[3] Joseph Freeman, *An American Testament* (New York: Farrar, 1936), p. 50.

[4] Walter Lippmann, *A Preface to Politics*, p. 200, *passim*.

[5] Luhan, *Movers and Shakers*, p. 264; Mabel Dodge to Eastman, May 10, 1938, Eastman Mss; Randolph Bourne, quoted in Henry F. May, *The End of American Innocence* (New York: Knopf, 1959), p. 244.

[6] Eastman, *Enjoyment of Living*, p. 355.

[7] Reed, "Almost Thirty," pp. 18–19.

[8] Walter Lippmann, "Walling's 'Progressivism and After,' " *New Review*, II (June, 1914), 340–49; *id.*, "The IWW—Insurrection or Reaction," *New Review*, I (Aug., 1913), 701–06; *id.*, *A Preface to Politics*, p. 29; Eastman, *Love and Revolution*, p. 126.

[9] Dell, p. 251.

[10] W. J. Ghent, quoted in Fried, *Socialism in America*, p. 384.

[11] The "wit," quoted in Alfred Kazin, *On Native Grounds: An Interpretation of Modern American Prose Literature* (New York: Harcourt, 1942), p. 169.

[12] Charles E. Russell and J. G. Phelps Stokes, quoted in Fried, *Socialism in America*, pp. 508–09.

[13] Randolph Bourne, quoted in Freeman, *An American Testament*, pp. 105–06.

[14] Randolph Bourne, "A War Diary," in *War and the Intellectuals: Collected Essays, 1915–1919*, ed. Carl Resek (New York: Harper, 1964), pp. 36–47; Eastman, *Enjoyment of Living*, pp. 533–34; John Reed, "One Solid Month of Liberty," *The Masses*, IX (Sept., 1917), 5–6.

[15] Louis Fraina, *Revolutionary Socialism: A Study of Socialist Reconstruction* (New York: The Communist Press, 1918), pp. 62–63.

[16] Max Eastman, "The Religion of Patriotism," *The Masses*, IX (July, 1917), 8–12; Randolph Bourne, "The State," in *War and the Intellectuals*, pp. 65–104.

[17] Draper, *Roots of American Communism*, pp. 109–13.

[18] "The Communist Labor Party," *The Class Struggle* (editorial), III (Nov., 1919), 438–43.

[19] Max Schactman, "American Communism: A Re-Examination of the American Past," *The New International*, XXIII (Fall, 1957), 225.

[20] Reed, "Almost Thirty," pp. 8–18; Bertram D. Wolfe, *Strange Communists I Have Known* (New York: Bantam, 1967), pp. 11–35.

[21] Luhan, p. 189.

[22] Richard O'Connor and Dale L. Walker, *The Lost Revolutionary: A Biography of John Reed* (New York: Harcourt, 1967).

[23] Draper, pp. 284–93.

[24] Eastman, *Enjoyment of Living*, pp. xiv–xv, 15–18, 23–26.

[25] Freeman, p. 103.

[26] Eastman, *Love and Revolution*, pp. 14–16, 125–32; *id.*, *Marx and Lenin: The Science of Revolution* (New York: Albert Boni, 1927).

[27] Eastman, *Love and Revolution*, pp. 350–56; *id.*, *Since Lenin Died* (New York: Liveright, 1925); *id.*, *Leon Trotsky: The Portrait of a Youth* (New York: Greenberg, 1925), p. v.

[28] Eastman later brought together all his arguments in *Marxism is it Science* (New York: Norton, 1940).

[29] Eastman helped Trotsky publish his works in the United States and he tried to help the exile obtain a visa to enter the country. But the two had a falling out over the issue of dialectical materialism. Eastman to Trotsky, July 9, 1929, August 14, 1933, Eastman mss; Trotsky to C. V. Calverton, November 4, 1932, Trotsky Archives, Houghton Library, Harvard University, Cambridge, Mass.

[30] Mario Savio, quoted in Lewis S. Feuer, *The Conflict of Generations: The Character and Significance of Student Movements* (New York: Basic Books, 1969), p. 503.

The Old Left 5

Every time I've encountered the Depression,
it has been used as a barrier and club. It's
been a counter-communication. Older people
use it to explain to me that I can't understand
anything. I didn't live through the Depression. They never say to me: We can't understand you because we didn't live through the
leisure society. All attempts at communica-
tion are totally blocked. All of a sudden
there's a generation gap. It's a frightening
thing.
   What they're saying is: For twenty years
I've starved and worked hard. You might
fight. It's very Calvinistic. Work, suffer,
have twenty lashes a day, and you can have
a bowl of bean soup.

Diane*

Do not let me hear,
Of the wisdom of old men.

T. S. Eliot†

But remember, also, young man: you are not
the first person who has ever been alone
and alone.

F. Scott Fitzgerald

In his *History of the Russian Revolution* Trotsky laid down three
conditions necessary for a successful seizure of power: "the ruling
classes, as a result of their practically manifested incapacity to get the

---

*A "twenty-seven-year-old journalist," in Studs Terkel, *Hard Times: An Oral History
of the Great Depression.*
†From "East Coker" in "Four Quartets" in COLLECTED POEMS 1909–1962 by T. S.
Eliot, © 1963 by Harcourt Brace Jovanovich, Inc. © 1963 by Faber and Faber Ltd. Reprinted with permission of Harcourt Brace Jovanovich and Faber and Faber Ltd.

country out of its blind alley, lose confidence in themselves"; the lower classes develop "a bitter hostility to the existing order and a readiness to venture upon the most heroic efforts and sacrifice in order to bring the country out upon an upward road"; and "discontent of . . . intermediate layers [roughly the middle classes], their disappointment with the policy of the ruling class, their impatience and indignation, their readiness to support a bold initiative on the part of the proletariat, constitute the third political premise of a revolution."[1]

THE DEPRESSION AND COMMUNISM

During the Depression, America never came close to meeting these conditions. Amid the panic following the economic crash in the fall of 1929, only the capitalists fulfilled their historic mission by losing faith in themselves and becoming, through their short-sighted economic policies, their own gravediggers. The proletariat failed to show any "bold initiative," while the American middle class remained as timid and conservative as ever. There was much hopeful talk in the left-wing press of "revolution," but those who actually went to the masses found only misery and confusion. The montage that emerges out of the photographic essays of Dorothea Lange, the reportage of James Agee, the novels of John Steinbeck, Horace McCoy, and James T. Farrell, and the microsociology of Helen and Robert Lynd makes a haunting picture of people with blank faces and broken spirits, of human bodies bent over like staring question marks. Watching the bonus marches and bread lines, the starvation of rural migrant workers and the dissolution of urban families, Americans became apprehensive. Occasionally they grew angry and even violent, but just as often they turned their resentment back upon themselves. For most Americans felt the Depression as an individual, not a class experience, and, since they considered unemployment a sign of personal failure, the idle hands blamed not society but themselves. This was the "invisible scar" that the Depression generation would bear almost the rest of its life.[2] Historically, what was remarkable about the public during the Depression was not the extent of its protest and sense of conflict but the extent of its patience and sense of contrition.

The extent of this psychic wound indicates how much America's working classes had absorbed the values of capitalist individualism.

61 and 62 *(right)* Migrant farm workers, once farm owners, en route to another job during the Depression. *(below)* A group of unemployed sit in dejection before their shack on New York City's waterfront.

Had there been a viable Left in the 1920's propounding a socialist consciousness among the workers, the story of radicalism in the 1930's might have been different. Nevertheless, although the depression may have vindicated DeLeon, American intellectuals also felt vindicated as they watched Wall Street collapse like a house of cards. "To the writers and artists of my generation," wrote Edmund Wilson, "who had grown up in the Big Business era and had always resented its barbarism, its crowding-out of everything they cared about, these years were not depressing but stimulating. One couldn't help being exhilarated at the sudden unexpected collapse of that stupid gigantic fraud. It gave us a new sense of freedom; and it gave us a new sense of power to find ourselves still carrying on while the bankers, for a change, were taking a beating."[3]

It is difficult to speak of the Old Left as a single generational entity. The radicals of the thirties differed in age, ideology, social background, cultural sensibility, life style, and political commitment. Among literary intellectuals alone there were at least three distinct groups. First were the veteran radicals of the 1920's, a disparate band of intellectuals who wrote on a variety of subjects for V. F. Calverton's *Modern Quarterly.* The isolated radical intelligentsia of the 1920's also found a sounding board in the *New Masses,* started in 1926 by its combative editor Mike Gold. A heavy-handed polemicist, Gold loved to affect the unwashed mien of the proletariat, and he relished chomping on foul, three-cent Italian cigars and spitting profusely on the floor while he denounced as "pansies" such writers as T. S. Eliot. A second circle of radical writers rose to prominence in the early 1930's with the publication of *Partisan Review.* Considerably younger than veteran radicals like Calverton and Eastman were such writers as Phillip Rahv, William Phillips, Dwight Macdonald, and F. W. Dupee, the brilliant, college-bred intelligentsia of the Depression. Urbane, steeped in modern literature and philosophy, these New York intellectuals had no illusions about a proletarian cultural renaissance and refused to cast aside the intellectual heritage of the recent past. A third group of writers who were part of the Old Left were cultural refugees from the 1920's. Novelists and essayists like John Dos Passos and Malcolm Cowley had been survivors of the celebrated "lost generation" that had expatriated to

Europe to flee the emotional and esthetic sterility of America, "an old bitch gone in the teeth" (Ezra Pound). Many of these exiles returned with a feeling of guilty relief. In the 1920's they had turned inward and lost themselves either in an abstruse cultivation of literary craft or in a stylized search for personal salvation. Attempting to create new values, some found in Hemingway's stoical characters a code of courage that enabled man to endure a violent and absurd world and confront the nothingness ("nada") of existence. Many emerged from the privatized intellectual life of the twenties with a shameful sense of their egotistical and ineffectual response to the alienation of bourgeois existence. F. Scott Fitzgerald, reflecting with painful honesty upon his own "crack-up," believed that his failure to develop a "political conscience" was partly responsible for his loss of identity ("So there was not an 'I' anymore"). Fitzgerald's conviction that his own nervous breakdown was symptomatic of America's social crisis revealed a strain of guilt, felt by many writers, that their former lives had been shallow and selfish—as the generation of the thirties had judged them. "I think that my happiness, or my talent for self-delusion or what you will, was an exception," confessed Fitzgerald. "It was not the natural thing but the unnatural—unnatural as the Boom; and my recent experience parallels the wave of despair that swept over the nation when the Boom was over."[4]

Fitzgerald's generation looked back upon the twenties as if it were a joyless quest for joy. The fashionable despair of Eliot's *The Waste Land* could not sustain the expatriates, and well before the Depression they began to ache for a positive faith and a new social ethic. In contrast to the earlier generation of Marxists, like Calverton and Gold and the later generation of writers like Rahv and Phillips, the conversion of America's lost generation to radicalism meant the end of a lonely cultural odyssey and the beginning of a new political life. For the Old Left in general, however, the appeals of communism are explained more by the realities of the thirties than by the experience of the twenties. The Depression sensitized intellectuals to life at the lower levels of society. The misery of the unemployed and uprooted, the exploitation of the blacks, and the desperate struggle of the workingman made capitalism all the more atrocious and communism all the more attractive.

63 and 64   A poster by Fred Ellis, American radical artist of the 1930's, depicts "two civilizations"—America *(left)* and the Soviet Union *(facing page)*.

But the spectacle of human suffering did not in itself account for the widespread radicalization of the American intelligentsia. Injustice and exploitation had existed long before the Depression. The Depression made poverty more visible, but it was communism that made it intolerable.

Central to the appeal of communism was the mighty image of Soviet Russia. In the two years following the Bolshevik Revolution in 1917, the *New York Times* predicted, in ninety-one different editorials, the collapse or near-collapse of Soviet communism. With the collapse of western capitalism a decade later, the image of Russia changed dramatically. As President Hoover seemed to lapse into a funk of indecision, and Stalin celebrated the "success" of his Five-Year Plans, even industrialists like Henry Ford and financiers like Thomas Lamont praised

Russia and advocated bestowing America's formal diplomatic recognition. To Left intellectuals especially, the young Soviet republic appeared as a model of human brotherhood surrounded by a selfish and aggressive capitalist world. The spectrum of admirers encompassed not only the small American communist Left but the larger liberal Center as well—fellow travelers who supported the idea of communism but did not join the party, and Russian sympathizers who praised Soviet economic achievements but rejected communist ideology. Only a few zealous radicals believed that Soviet communism could be transplanted to America and the Bolshevik Revolution duplicated. What the noncommunist Left wanted to borrow from Russia was the new and bold idea of centralized economic planning. In the liberal *New Republic* and *Nation,* and in the journals of the Left, an image emerged of a dy-

65 *Eternal City*, Peter Blume's allegory of fascism. Many saw communism as the only bulwark against the depicted threat of fascism.

namic country blazing with smoking factories and churning tractors run by grim-jawed Russian men with enormous biceps and smiling peasant girls with big, honest calves.

The contrast between Russia's highly propagandized economic progress and America's continued economic stagnation was one source of communism's sway over the intellectual's imagination. Another was the image of communism as the solitary bulwark against fascism. Hitler's accession to power in January 1933 hardly troubled the CP, which accepted the Comintern's judgment that fascism merely signified capitalism's last stage. Yet fascism seemed so barbaric and irrational that most intellectuals could only watch in stunned disbelief as "civilized" Germany succumbed to it. While intellectuals pondered the fate of western democracy, the communist press now claimed that the triumph of the Nazis in Germany exposed the hollowness of liberalism everywhere. Some discerning Marxists, like Sidney Hook and many of

114

the followers of Trotsky, rejected this argument. Yet the communist interpretation carried great emotional appeal, for fascism symbolized everything intellectuals hated: political demagogy, capitalist decadence, militarism, and imperialism. Moreover, in analyzing the causes of fascism, some liberal intellectuals found it difficult to admit that the middle classes, previously regarded as the driving force of American progressivism, comprised the social backbone of fascist movements. The communist thesis that fascism evolved from "monopoly capitalism" was far more satisfying. But whether intellectuals saw fascism as a plot of industrialists alone or as a popular mass movement, two conclusions could be drawn: that fascism could evolve from capitalism was final proof that capitalism must be abolished; that fascism could eliminate the Left in Europe was final proof that the Left in America must organize against it. Organizing against it meant coming to terms with the CP.

A third source of communism's strength in the 1930's was that byzantine organization, the CPUSA—the Communist Party, U.S.A. In reality, few intellectuals became official Party members because the CP demanded a loyalty that confused discipline with indoctrination, its leaders frequently treated intellectuals with disdain, and its internal doctrinal disputes often took on the arid flavor of medieval scholasticism. Even so, intellectuals had to admit that the CP possessed an effective organization, offered a clear program of action, and enjoyed the blessing of the Soviet Union. The CP's leadership may have been ruthless, but intellectuals saw the ruling classes as much more ruthless and more dangerous. Combatting capitalism required more than sweetness and light, and in the early thirties many writers, even those who did not join, found in the CP a source of political strength and comradeship with the mass of workers who possessed the means of overthrowing the existing order. The playwright John Howard Lawson told Dos Passos that though Mike Gold might call him a "bourgeois Hamlet," "my own plan is to work very closely with the communists in the future, to get into some strike activity, and to accept a good deal of discipline in doing so. It seems to me the only course open to people like ourselves." "It is a bad world in which we live, and so even the revolutionary movement is anything but what (poetically and philosophically

115

speaking) it 'ought' to be," Granville Hicks was told in a letter from a communist friend. "It seems nothing but grime and stink and sweat and obscene noises and the language of beasts. But surely this is what *history* is. It is just not made by gentlemen and scholars."[5]

Far more important than the CP was the influence of Marxism upon American thinkers. Actually, most Left intellectuals were only "Marxists of the heart," radicals who sensed that Marxism was right because they knew that capitalism was wrong. But several serious scholars, mainly those who wrote for the short-lived *Marxist Quarterly,* attempted to master Marxism as a philosophy of history and as a theory of economics. In doing so they tried, significantly, to make Marxism compatible with America's intellectual tradition. The philosopher Sidney Hook interpreted Marxism as a "radical humanism" that shared with American pragmatism a common naturalistic theory of knowledge; the historian Louis Hacker reinterpreted the American Revolution as a study in imperialism and the Civil War as a class struggle; and the social scientist Lewis Corey saw parallels in Marx's and Veblen's analysis of class behavior.[6] The attempt to make Marxism the logical extension of traditional progressive values may have set political theory back fifty years. But Marxism did restore meaning and purpose to life by offering a sense of historical direction, a method of class analysis, and an organic vision that dared to be monistic. In an age when all truths seemed relative and fragmentary, Marxism could provide a rare glimpse of the totality of existence, an exciting synthesis that broke down the classical dualisms between self and society, idealism and realism, contemplation and action, art and life.

Ultimately Marxist communism appealed to intellectuals because, as Daniel Aaron noted, "it seemed a science as well as an ethic, because it explained and foretold as well as inspired."[7] The overwhelming desire of intellectuals to believe that history was on their side also suggests the emotional value of Marxism for the generation of the thirties. For Marxism resolved the contradictory tensions that lay at the heart of the Old Left: professing a pragmatic devotion to William James's pluralistic universe, American radicals devoted themselves to a Marxist world view that was fixed and predetermined; claiming to have thrown off the sentimental idealism of the past, they embraced a "realistic" doctrine demanding the idealism of sacrifice and commitment; seeing themselves as men of ideas, they admired men of action; believing in truth, they respected power. Clearly it was not the intellectual content of Marxism that converted many American intellectuals to radicalism. "It was not merely the power of ideology that bound one to the Movement," recalled Irving Howe, who had taken to radicalism at the adventurous age of fourteen:

> No, what I think held young people to the Movement was the sense that they had gained, not merely a "purpose" in life but, far more important, a coherent perspective upon everything that was happening to us. And this perspective was something rather different from, a good deal more practical and immediate than, Marxist ideology; it meant the capacity for responding quickly and with a comforting assurance to events. The Movement gave us a language of response and gesture, the security of a set orientation—perhaps impossible to a political tendency that lacked an ideology but not quite to be identified with ideology as such. It felt good "to know." One revelled in the innocence and arrogance of knowledge, for even in our inexpert hands Marxism could be a powerful analytic tool and we could nurture the feeling that, whether other people realized it or not, we enjoyed a privileged relationship to history. . . .
>
> But there is a more fundamental reason for the appeal of the Movement. Marxism involves a profoundly *dramatic* view of human experience. With its stress upon inevitable conflicts, apocalyptic climaxes, ultimate moments, hours of doom, and shining tomorrows, it appealed deeply to our imaginations. We felt that we were always on the rim of heroism, that the mockery we might suffer at the moment would turn to vindication in the future, that our loyalty to principle would be rewarded by the grateful masses of tomorrow. The principle of classic drama, peripeteia or the sudden reversal of fortune, we stood upon its head quite as Marx was supposed to have done to Hegel; and then it became for us a crux of our political system. The moment would come, our leaders kept assuring us and no doubt themselves, if only we did not flinch, if only we were ready to remain a tiny despised minority, if only we held firm to our sense of destiny. It was this pattern of drama which made each moment of our participation seem so rich with historical meaning.[8]

In contrast to the desperate need for a coherent orientation, the mood of the earlier Left was far less anxious and far more confident. The 1913 Lyrical Left found in history what the Old Left could find only in a visceral ideology. Before the war the exciting rise of socialism in the

United States and in Europe enabled the young radicals to issue declarations that rang with the certainty of truth. Moreover, for the most part the Lyrical Left was made up of humanitarians and pacifists, "tender" radicals who knew nothing of the surreal world of totalitarianism and terror that was to emerge in the 1930's. Nor did the earlier radicals witness the decay of European social democracy into petrified party bureaucracies, the bastardization of radical syndicalist ideas into fascist ideologies, and the grotesque betrayals by Stalin. With its vague, quasi-anarchist illusions and festive spirit, the Lyrical Left saw itself standing at the dawn of a new era in which intellectuals at last could live without compromising their devotion to truth, beauty, and justice.

The difference between the Lyrical Left and the Old Left is the difference between innocence and experience. To the radicals of the thirties, the Depression may have first seemed like the beginning of "America's October Revolution." But the unexpected triumph of fascism in Europe caused them to reconsider the resiliency of capitalism and the cunning nature of power. After 1935 few American radicals believed that democratic socialism was the only historical alternative to capitalism. Still more chastening was the choice of comrades: since liberals in America had failed to prevent the revival of corporate capitalism under the New Deal, and since socialists in Europe had failed to prevent the rise of fascism, the Old Left was presented with the cruel alternative of Stalinism or fascism. Even the many writers who refused to accept this myth of the false alternative realized that political choices were not clear and easy. That the choice for and against humanity would involve the trauma of deciding between two forms of totalitarianism, that one would have to choose the bad against the worse, was an experience almost unknown to the Lyrical Left.

The Old Left also differed from its predecessor in respect to social background and intellectual orientation. The major figures of the Lyrical Left, having been brought up in small towns in the midwest or rural northeast, found much of their earlier inspiration in the native legacy of cultural radicalism, especially in Thoreau's defiant individualism and Whitman's cosmic collectivism. The Old Left intellectuals, many of Russian Jewish or east European ancestry, born in New York City's ghettos, were more inclined to turn away from American in-

NEW MASSES

MAY 1933
15 Cents

Scottsboro
Louis Berg

I Saw the Nazis
Edward Dahlberg

Greenwich
Village Types
Joseph Freeman

66 Typical *New Masses* cover, with drawing by Gropper.

tellectual traditions and look elsewhere for an inspiring radical ideology. Marxism, which seemed so uniquely a product of the European mind, emerged as a more natural ideology to the sons and daughters of immigrants. The distinction between the two radical generations can also be seen in the differences between the old *Masses* and the *New Masses*. The former infused the Left with a hearty spirit of adventure and innovation, the latter imbued it with an arid strain of dogmatism. Indeed, the *New Masses* attempted to burn out of the American Left every vestige of its bohemian past. Two victims were Eastman (ironical-

119

ly, "anti-bohemian" himself) and Floyd Dell, veterans of the Lyrical Left. Eastman continued to argue that cultural freedom was the quintessence of radicalism, and Dell continued to believe that radicalism could be a sensual affair as well as a serious struggle. "When you go to Russia," Dell asked a writer, "I hope you will write me about their new sexual conventions in great detail." But *New Masses* editor Mike Gold dismissed Eastman's concern for artistic freedom as a "Platonic" delusion, while Dell's obsession with sex was that of a sick bourgeois intellectual who "became the historian of the phallic-hunting girls of Greenwich Village." Still the sybarite, Dell later remarked that in the *New Masses'* cartoons "the women always had square breasts—which seems to me to denote a puritanical and fanatical hatred of women as the source of pleasure." Gold and Calverton refused to see, said Dell, that sex for him was his "manumission from the bondage of a preoccupation with a Grand Economic Explanation of Everything, which is rigor mortis to the mind."[9]

Compared to the sensuous emotions that animated the Lyrical Left, the Old Left was driven by a sodden intensity born of the anxieties and insecurities of the Depression. The strident ideological debates and polemics merely reflected the fratricidal sectarianism of the period. They also suggest a further contrast between the Lyrical Left and the Old Left. To a large extent, the former was made up of rebels, the latter of revolutionaries (or those who, under the spell of Marxism, briefly saw themselves as revolutionaries). The rebel rises as an individual in opposition to all sources of oppression; the revolutionary focuses all his antagonisms upon one object and channels all his energy into one movement. The rebel desires to assault traditional structure and authority; the revolutionary desires to destroy in order to create a specific new social order. The rebel has a Quixotic world view, skeptical of "closed systems"; the revolutionary has an "organically" integrated world view in which "totality" is everything (Georg Lukacs). And the rebel, to borrow Arthur Koestler's useful distinction, has the capacity to change causes; the revolutionary does not.[10] Actually, few radicals in the thirties were true revolutionaries. Nevertheless, communist doctrine did give them the illusion that they were revolutionaries ready to storm the barricades when the hour of truth presented itself. Communism served to constrict the perspectives of radicalism and to confine the intellectual's passion to a single cause. "Individual rebellion has passed out of me," wrote Joseph Freeman, who made the transition from the Lyrical to the Old Left, "and now I would like more than anything else to be a disciplined worker in the movement."[11] The revolutionary movement became the great cause of the Old Left. When it failed, many intellectuals who threw their bodies and souls into it emerged, not merely disillusioned as in the case of the earlier Left, but so bitter, exhausted, and guiltridden that they abandoned all causes. To comprehend their retreat from radicalism requires a brief sketch of the unhappy history of the Old Left.

THE POPULAR FRONT

Ideologically, the Old Left encompassed both socialism and communism, and the tensions that had earlier divided the two re-emerged in the thirties. The socialists organized around the older Socialist Labor Party and Socialist Party and the new American Workers Party. In 1934 the AWP was established to forge a radical movement independent of both the SP and CP. Led by the Dutch-born preacher A. J. Muste, the AWP refrained from dogmatic formulations of economic problems, organized the unemployed in the small industrial towns of the Ohio Valley, and attracted several independent radicals who wanted to avoid repeating socialist and communist tactical mistakes. Meanwhile the SLP continued to attack the reformism of the democratic socialists and the centralism of the communists, thus remaining true to DeLeon and as isolated as ever from the mainstream of American radicalism. The SP itself could poll only 903,000 votes (2 percent of the total vote) when it ran Norman Thomas for President in 1932. (Debs polled 6 percent in 1912). Moreover, the party was sick with factionalism. With a membership of roughly 15,000, the SP was made up of older Jewish trade union leaders, a small core of Protestant pacifists, and young students who formed the League for Industrial Democracy. The younger militants often sided with Thomas and challenged the leadership of old-guard socialists like Hillquit. Aside from internal difficulties, the SP faced two new challenges in the thirties: the gradual winning over of

121

workers in the coal mines, steel mills, and clothing factories by the New Deal's labor reforms; and the seductiveness of the wealth-sharing panaceas of Dr. Francis Townsend, Huey Long, and Upton Sinclair.

To the Left intellectuals, democratic socialism seemed stale and timid. "Becoming a socialist right now," wrote Dos Passos in 1932, "would have just about the same effect on anybody as drinking a bottle of near-beer."[12] To intellectuals who wanted a party more audacious than the SP but not quite as centralized as the CP, the only choices were two communist splinter groups whose influence among radical writers was perhaps the one consolation of their lonely isolation. The Lovestonites and the Trotskyists, both expelled from the CP in the 1920's, still regarded themselves as the only genuine communists in America. The former group, led by Jay Lovestone, Bertram D. Wolfe, and Will

67 Socialist Party presidential nominee Norman Thomas campaigns in Philadelphia in 1932, when the party won 2 percent of the vote.

Herberg, was often called the CP of the Right Opposition, just as the latter, led by James P. Cannon, James Burnham, and Max Schactman, called itself the CP of the Left Opposition. After failing to win the Comintern's endorsement in 1929, the Lovestonites continued to stress their conservative thesis of "American exceptionalism," which criticized communists for applying Marxist-Leninist ideas mechanically to the peculiar conditions of America instead of creatively adapting them. Sharing with the Lovestonites an opposition to Stalinism, the Trotskyists claimed that only they represented the true Left, and that therefore they, the real Leninist revolutionaries, would soon displace the official CP and reconstitute a new, authentic party and a new Communist International. Although these two opposition factions had together less than a thousand members, the Lovestonites' *Workers Age* and the Trotskyists' *New International* gave the Left a variety of refreshing and usually discerning viewpoints. Later in the thirties the Trotskyists won increasing support among several literary intellectuals who could no longer tolerate the Comintern-dominated *The Communist* and the CP's *Daily Worker.*

In the early thirties, however, the communists commanded most attention. In 1932 the League of Professional Groups published *Culture and Crisis,* calling upon writers, doctors, scientists, artists, and teachers to vote for William Z. Foster and James Ford, the presidential candidates of the CP. Those who heaped contempt upon the reformist SP and gave their allegiance to the revolutionary CP included many of America's most notable writers and scholars. What originally attracted intellectuals to communism was the confidence and aggressiveness of the CP, now intoxicated by the so-called "third period" of the international communist movement (the first, 1919–21, witnessed the abortive communist insurrections in Hungary and Bavaria; the second, 1922–28, saw Russia acknowledging the stabilization of world capitalism and making friendly diplomatic overtures to the West). The policy of the third period fitted the mood of the early Depression, for it asserted that the time for a revolutionary offensive had now been reached in the development of world capitalism. This new strategy caused the CP to shift tactics on the labor question. Previously the CP had accepted the Comintern's judgment that the development of a radical consciousness

68   Police and Teamsters Union strikers clash in Minneapolis in a scene that became increasingly familiar during the Depression years. The American Trotskyists, although small in number, had some influence in the Teamsters Union.

among American workers would be slow. Now the CP reversed itself and made every effort to penetrate and capture the labor movement by taking over strikes wherever possible, and, after the economic crash, by setting up unemployment councils and again instructing each of its members to "turn his face to the factory. " The CP also launched a policy of dual unionism, under which, as the Depression deepened, rival communist unions or locals were established in clothing, textile, coal, tool and die, restaurant, shoe, and automobile industries. Later, when John L. Lewis broke from the AFL in 1936 and formed the CIO, communists were able to move in on the ground floor and establish a base in more than a dozen CIO affiliates, including the strategic longshore, maritime, and transport unions.

It is enormously difficult to ascertain the exact influence of the CP in the labor movement during the Depression. The New Left historian Staughton Lynd has recorded the glowing recollections of several CIO veterans praising the organizational efforts of communists. The more thorough research of Theodore Draper, however, suggests the limitations of communist influence on labor in general. The CP, for example, made an all-out effort to win over southern textile workers and miners in the brutal strikes at Gastonia, North Carolina, and in Harlan County, Kentucky. But the failure of these poorly organized, ill-timed strikes was a calamity for the workers, who, always suspicious of the "atheistic" doctrines of communism, became openly hostile to any further efforts at communist infiltration. Nevertheless, communists who entered the South were the first to risk their lives attempting to expose the appalling poverty and working conditions, and they succeeded in gaining the support of a number of important intellectuals, including the novelists Theodore Dreiser and John Dos Passos, who publicized to the nation the desperate plight of the southern workers.[13]

Energy and determination brought success to the communists. The organization men of the American Left, communists were always available to hand out leaflets on bitter cold mornings, to sit out dreary meetings until they had won their point, never shirking the boring, dirty work of radicalism. Perhaps the one potential ally the communists

69 Striking textile workers demonstrate at Gastonia, North Carolina, in 1929.

failed to organize was the black American. The painful economic distress of the Depression made the black American receptive to radicalism, and black writers like W. E. B. DuBois and George Padmore had read enough Marx to show their brothers that racial suppression and economic exploitation were related phenomena. But the CP failed to arouse a mass movement of black workers and intellectuals because of three strategic errors. First was its formulation of the "Black Belt" doctrine, which, in its attempt to keep the class question separate from the color question, proposed a separate "Negro republic" in the South, a move that scarcely met the immediate needs of black Americans. Second was its expedient handling of the Scottsboro trials of nine black youths falsely accused of rape, which offended the NAACP and other black groups. And third was its defense of the Soviet Union's policy of supplying oil to fascist Italy during the Ethiopian War despite black protests.[14]

Communists enjoyed more success with young Americans. During the Depression, youths suffered great hardships. Almost one-third could not find work, and those from lower-income families had to quit school to make ends meet at home. Even those who managed to graduate from college found themselves a "locked-out" generation, an unwanted

70 A comment on Southern racial oppression in the *Daily Worker* of 1927. The gun-carrying low-class white says: "You can't vote, yer too ignorant."

intelligentsia who were glad to find work anywhere, even digging ditches on a government Works Progress Administration project—a sight that could both delight and sadden hardened laborers. One college newspaper celebrated its graduating class in an "Ode to Higher Education":

> I sing in praise of college
> Of M.A.'s and Ph.D.'s
> But in pursuit of knowledge
> We are starving by degrees.[15]

The most important radical youth organizations were the Young Communist League and its campus counterpart the National Student League, which had thriving branches at City College, Brooklyn College, and Hunter College (all New York City schools), the University of Chicago and the University of Wisconsin, and, on the west coast, Berkeley and the University of California, Los Angeles. After visiting campuses, even conservative critics in Congress were forced to admit what most professors knew all along: that YCL members were often the brightest and most articulate students. Young activists fought for academic freedom, raised funds for striking coal miners, rushed to the defense of dismissed radical professors, and, while college presidents fretted over continued support of wealthy benefactors, talked of bringing the class struggle into the classroom. Communists also participated in the upsurge of pacifism among students of the thirties. The greatest display of solidarity occurred on April 13, 1934, when in New York City alone between 15,000 and 25,000 students walked out of their 11:00 A.M. classes in a massive antiwar strike (estimates for the entire country varied between 500,000 and 1,000,000).

For the sensitive young, becoming a communist could mean both a painful and an exhilarating break with parents and relatives. One father, H. Bedford-Jones, published an article in the conservative magazine *Liberty* under the hair-raising title, "Will Communists Get Our Girls in College?" claiming he had learned from his daughter how shaggy radicals seduced and subverted innocent coeds. The following week the *New Masses* responded with an article by the daughter of Bedford-Jones, "My Father Is a Liar!"[16]

The CP, which in the twenties had its roots in the immigrant working classes, began reaching out to other sections of American society
in the thirties. The results of its recruitment drives were remarkable.
Membership rose from 7500 in 1930 to 55,000 in 1938, with perhaps
30,000 more unregistered members in various youth groups and trade
unions.[17] The skill and ability with which communists carried out
organizational campaigns is not the only explanation for their success.
Equally important was the new strategy of the Popular Front, which
replaced the disastrous policies of the third period, described above.

The heady expectations of the third period rested largely on the theory
of "social fascism," a notion first developed in the early 1920's by
European communists in an effort to undermine the social democrats
in Germany and elsewhere. In accordance with this thesis communists
were instructed to turn "class against class" so that in the end only two
classes (the proletariat and the bourgeoisie) would confront one another
in mortal combat. In order to discredit liberals and socialists, the CP
took the position that all those who were not communists were class
enemies and that liberal-social democracy and fascism were expressions of the same repressive bourgeois state, the only difference being
that the former was "masked" and the latter "naked." In Germany,
communists thus scorned the socialists' attempt to oppose Hitler's
maneuver to power, and in the United States communists attacked
Norman Thomas and President Roosevelt as "social fascists." The communist strategy presumed that fascism reflected capitalism's "final
crisis"; hence, whatever tactic would expedite Hitler's advent to power
was a victory for communism ("After Hitler, Our Turn!").[18] But when
Hitler consolidated power and made it clear that fascism was anything
but a transitory phenomenon, and when Roosevelt seemed able to sal-
vage American capitalism, the theory of social fascism had to be
abandoned. Instead of predicting fascism's imminent collapse, communists now described it as an imminent threat. The USSR responded
by joining the League of Nations and signing a mutual defense pact
with France, and the Comintern announced the new policy of the
Popular Front.

The Popular Front of 1935 represented a complete *volte face*. Whereas
the CP previously had insisted on class struggle, it now called for

collaboration with the bourgeoisie. It had formerly exalted the Soviet system of government; now it extolled the virtues of American democracy. It once had preached internationalism; now it praised nationalism. American communists embraced the new course without so much as a blush of embarrassment, hailing socialists as fellow comrades and praising Roosevelt as an enlightened statesman. Communists now became respectable, and the CP began to seem like an evangelical church that opened its door to all believers. The attempt to make communism into "Twentieth Century Americanism" also meant that the less acrid works of Jefferson, Lincoln, and Thomas Paine had to be stressed over Marxist-Leninist writings. At CP meetings the stars and stripes could be seen above the red flag. Patriotism, the refuge of scoundrels, became the haven of Stalinists. Even young communists sounded like clean-cut all-Americans:

> Some people have the idea that a YCLer is politically minded, that nothing outside politics means anything. Gosh no. They have a few simple problems. There is the problem of getting good men on the baseball team, of dating girls, etc. We go to shows, parties, dances, and all that. In short, the YCL and its members are no different from other people except that we believe in dialectical materialism as a solution to all problems.[19]

The Popular Front had immense appeal to many elements of the noncommunist Left, especially to liberals who had always urged a common front against fascism and who found themselves in the mid-thirties without a viable ideology. By blurring the distinction between Marxism and progressivism and by de-emphasizing revolution, the Popular Front also gave liberals the impression that they had convinced communists to come to their collective senses. Speaking of CP members, Upton Sinclair boasted: "I do not mean to be egotistical and imply that they have taken my advice, but it is a fact that they are now saying and doing what I urged them for many years to say and do: to support and cooperate with the democratic peoples."[20]

Caught up in the spirit of the Popular Front, much of the American Left accepted the Stalinist interpretation of two momentous events that began in 1936: the Spanish Civil War and the Moscow Purge trials. Approximately 3200 Americans joined the Abraham Lincoln Brigade to fight for the imperiled Spanish republic. The choice of Lincoln's

129

71 *Guernica* (1937), Picasso's famous expression of the anguish of his homeland under

name was typical of the Popular Front strategy, for to the Stalinists it signaled that the duty of American volunteers was to preserve the republic, not to turn the war into a social revolution. At the same time, however, the real forces of the Left in Spain were the Trotskyists (POUM), and especially the anarchists, who were establishing collective farms and workers' councils in an attempt to transform the civil war into a genuine revolution. But the Comintern, possibly fearing that a revolutionary Spain would arouse the wrath of western nations, ordered Spanish communists to put down a popular uprising in Barcelona and to liquidate several anarchist leaders. In the United States only a handfull of isolated anti-Stalinists publicized the repression. Dos Passos, one of the few literary intellectuals to take a stand, broke with his close

Franco during the Spanish Civil War.

friend Hemingway and declared that a crime is a crime whether committed by the Left or Right.[21]

While news from Spain upset a few radical intellectuals, reports from Moscow convulsed the entire Left. Stalin's systematic purge of thousands of former bolshevik leaders, some of them heroes in the eyes of American radicals, remains one of the most enigmatic episodes in the twentieth century. Branded as traitors or fascist agents, the accused often confessed in open court to crimes they could not possibly have committed. They did so knowing a firing squad awaited them no matter how they pleaded. From 1936 to 1938 the American Left was stunned by the eerie proceedings. Most socialists, suspicious as ever of Stalin, denounced the trials; and the Trotskyists, fearing a bloodbath against

72 Three of the more than 3000 Americans who made up the Abraham Lincoln Brigade, which fought on the Loyalist side in the Spanish Civil War. From left, John Gates, Robert Thompson, and Dave Doran. Thompson's death in 1965 sparked a controversy over whether a communist—though a Second World War hero—could be buried in Arlington National Cemetery.

anti-Stalinists everywhere, sought to expose the farce. Trotskyists in America succeeded in gaining the support of philosopher John Dewey, who headed a commission of inquiry that went to Mexico to obtain from the exiled Trotsky testimony with which to conduct a "counter-trial" outside the USSR. But when the commission defended Trotsky and published the book *Not Guilty,* a storm of controversy erupted. Immediately 150 "American Progressives" signed a statement supporting the Moscow trials. Although motives were complex and varied, those intellectuals who condoned the trials generally feared the collapse of the Popular Front. In their minds Trotsky preached world revolution, class struggle, and opposition to democracy; hence it was Stalin's enemies who played into the hands of the fascists, undermined the strength of the Soviet Union, and thereby endangered a united front on the Left. But even those communists who opposed the Popular Front justified the purges by appealing to the goddess of history. Citing the political trials that occurred during the French Revolution, Jay Lovestone concluded:

132

"In effect, we practically ignore the charges, refutations and counter-charges, and ask ourselves: *Which tendency was carrying forward the interests of the revolution and which was obstructing it?* Some may be shocked at this utterly 'unmoral' approach but it seems to be the approach of history!"[22]

A few years later, after an alleged Stalinist agent in Mexico killed the heavily guarded Trotsky with an ice-ax, embittered American Trotskyists accused other radicals of supporting Stalin because he had power while Trotsky had only the most brilliant mind of the century. Had radical intellectuals admitted the monstrous hoax of the show trials, they would have had to question the moral distinction between communism and fascism and admit that truth was no longer *the* virtue of the Left. "One of the worst drawbacks of being a Stalinist at the present time," wrote Edmund Wilson in 1937, "is that you have to defend so many falsehoods." "It is difficult for me to believe that you entered an alliance with fascism," Waldo Frank complained to Trotsky, "but it is equally difficult for me to believe that Stalin carried out such horrible frame-ups." To concede the terror of the trials required an ad-

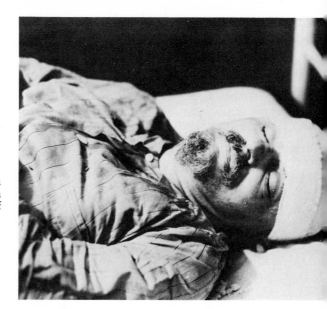

73 Leon Trotsky, dead in a Mexico City hospital after an attack by a presumed agent of Joseph Stalin.

mission of one's own naiveté for having believed that Marxism would somehow solve the problem of human aggression. With excruciating self-analysis, Frank later asked: "Could the vision within Marxism not be deepened? Not be made true? This was my hope, and my strategy. In my journal of those days I wrote: 'I collaborate with the revolutionists not expecting them to understand me: the bad logic of their dogmatic empiricism prevents that. But I must serve and understand them; and part of my service is to let them exploit me.'" Years afterwards, some Left intellectuals would justify their support of Stalin on the grounds that Hitler was the greater threat and Stalin the only ruler willing and able to crush the Third Reich. Even so, those who remained silent emerged from the decade with a conscience as pained as it was penitential. Reflecting on the private doubts, which he confided to a notebook rather than publish, Malcolm Cowley confessed: "That failure to publish led me into false situations, and later I would suffer for it— deservedly, I say to myself in private reckonings. When I add together these various sins of silence, self-protectiveness, inadequacy, and something close to moral cowardice, there appears to be reason for my feeling a sense of guilt about the second half of the decade."[23]

Thus, the Moscow trials created a crisis of conscience for the American Left. Although many could not bear the burden of truth, a number

74 and 75   Malcolm Cowley *(left)* and Granville Hicks *(right)* two of many Left intellectuals who repressed their doubts concerning the Soviet Union until late in the 1930's.

"THE MAROONED MAROON"

76 The *Washington Post* comments on the position of the American Communist Party in 1939. The communists, betrayed by the signing of the Russo-German nonaggression pact, were at the same time harassed by the House Un-American Activities Committee (the "Dies" Committee).

of important writers broke with the Popular Front and publicly condemned the Soviet government. Anti-Stalinist intellectuals formed the Committee for Cultural Freedom to protest the suppression of civil liberty in Russia as well as in Germany. While scholars began to apply the new term "totalitarian" to Russia along with Germany, Trotskyists debated whether Stalin's Russia could in any sense be considered a "workers' state," and, if not, whether they were obligated to defend it in case of war or adopt a policy of "revolutionary defeatism."[24] Stalin himself resolved the issue when the Soviet Union, on August 24, 1939, announced a neutrality and non-aggression pact with Nazi Germany. To wavering fellow travelers, the pact came as the final blow. Even communists, who might view the expedient maneuver as Stalin's answer to the Munich settlement, were shocked when they realized the Kremlin had given no hint of the negotiations. Thousands of members now left the CP, shaken by the thought that communism no less than fascism meant the end of morality in politics. During the height of the Popular Front, Russia stood for all that was good, rational, and progressive, and Germany for all that was evil, barbaric, and reactionary. The Nazi-Soviet pact killed the dream and, as W. H. Auden expressed it, "the clever hopes expired of a low dishonest decade." Granville Hicks, 135 an influential critic and literary editor of the *New Masses,* received a letter from a young woman protesting his resignation from the CP shortly after the pact:

> So it all comes to this: that your whole life previous to this time, all you underwent for the party, all the privations you seem willingly to have suffered when you could have had any post you wanted anywhere in the country, all this has gone up in a puff of smoke and lost its meaning. What for? You might just as well have taken it nice and easy and saved yourself the trouble. It might just as well never have happened. What a pity, to find one's life without meaning. What is left for you now?[25]

THE CRITIQUE OF MARXISM: LEGACY OF THE OLD LEFT

Finding their lives emptied of meaning, some radicals of the 1930's felt an overriding urge to come to grips with their past. A few intellectuals wrote novels or autobiographies in the hope that political truth might be generalized from personal experience. Most writers began to re-examine the faiths that had originally nourished and sustained their radicalism. In the process, Old Left intellectuals subjected Marxism to a critique in every area of human knowledge, and from their reconsiderations arose a new outlook toward the nature of American society and the nature of man.

Sociology: From Marx to Tocqueville

In the 1920's American intellectuals condemned capitalism on moral grounds. The despair with which many writers fled America's business culture merely revealed that few questioned the efficacy and durability of the free-enterprise system. In the thirties, however, capitalism was attacked not primarily because it was immoral but because it was irrational. Influenced by the Marxist theory of the inevitable clash of social classes, many writers believed they were witnessing the death agony of the old order as described in *Das Kapital:* Capitalists, in a frenzy of irrational competition, introduce labor-saving machinery and reduce further the workers' wages and buying power. As profits continue to shrink, unemployment rises, underconsumption spreads, small businesses go under, and, while the few remaining industrialists blindly continue to produce, the middle class realizes who its enemy is as it descends "gradually into the proletariat." After a series of worsening crises, "centralization of the means of production and socialization of labor at last reach a point where they become incompatible with their capitalist integument. This integument bursts asunder. The knell of capitalist private property sounds. The expropriators are expropriated."[26]

The idea that capitalism was prey to its own "contradictions" led Marxists to engage in an unrelieved dialogue on "inevitability." The dialogue was questioned when the collapse of capitalism failed to destroy the bourgeoisie and produce a polarization of classes in America. In *The Crisis of the Middle Class* (1935), Marxist Lewis Corey perceptively described the condition of the "petit bourgeoisie"; but as Corey would later admit, the old bourgeois stratum of small, victimized entrepreneurs declined only to be replaced by a "new middle class" of industrial technicians and middle-management employees. Gradually intellectuals began to sense that the "objective" concept of class, which viewed the worker only in his relation to the means of production, must be modified by an analysis of the worker's self-image in relation to his social and professional role. Anxieties about status helped explain why the "new middle class" would remain conservative and why the *déclassé* citizen could never bring himself to identify with the proletariat, as Marx had assumed. Moreover, when America failed to gravitate into two warring camps, Left intellectuals began to analyze the historical sources of America's peculiar social structure and value system in a search for the factors that had prevented the development of class consciousness. The key appeared to be in the writings of Alexis de Tocqueville, who a century earlier had described America as a homogenized and integrated social order where "equality of condition" was both an ideal and a reality. After the Second World War, ex-Marxist sociologists like Max Lerner and Seymour Martin Lipset would describe America as an "open class society" that was dynamic and mobile, bound together by common beliefs and values rooted in economic individualism and social conformity. This new outlook toward American society marked a dramatic shift from Marx's theory of class struggle and economic oppression imposed from above to Tocqueville's theory of class

137

diffusion and self-imposed social repression. In American sociology the concepts of status and consensus replaced those of class and conflict.[27]

Economics: From Marx to Keynes

If American society confounded Marxism, so did Franklin D. Roosevelt. It was the New Deal that gave hope to the American middle class and rescued capitalism from the cyclical manifestation of its death instinct. Roosevelt's programs failed to relieve the massive unemployment and revive the shaky economy—only the Second World War would bring about the huge government spending that restored stability —but the New Deal, with its social security measures and its recognition of labor's right to collective bargaining, eased the discontent of the lower and middle working classes. To the Left, the New Deal at first appeared a futile and chaotic experiment in class collaboration. The idea that a government could rise above the interests of the ruling class and respond to the pressures of organized labor and the majority of citizens (if not to the needs of the unorganized poor and forgotten minorities) was alien to the communist concept of the state. The Left also feared that the Roosevelt administration would be dominated by monopoly capitalists who would gradually transform America into a fascist corporate state. But Roosevelt's ability to steer a middle course between capitalist exploitation and socialist expropriation, while at the same time preserving traditional democratic institutions, seemed more attractive to disillusioned radicals who found a new respect for the politics of moderation as they watched the politics of extremism in Germany and Russia.

During the Second World War, moreover, even anticapitalist intellectuals were impressed by the great productive capacity of American enterprise, which was now being harnessed to destroy the awesome industrial might of Adolph Krupp and the Third Reich. After the war no one could speak of America's economy as irrational or contradictory in the realm of production. Yet instead of going beyond Marxism to a moral criticism of capitalism, some ex-radicals became fascinated by the government-spending policies of Keynesian economics and all but mesmerized by the magic of industrial growth. They now believed that

77 Passersby in a New York City street stare at an early NRA poster. The sight soon became commonplace throughout the nation.

78 Street-widening by the WPA during the Depression, one of the agency's many and varied programs.

the old socialist goal of equality could be ignored, since wealth no longer had to be redistributed but merely expanded. "There are no problems on the side of depression with which the American economy and polity cannot, if it must, contend," wrote John Kenneth Galbraith in 1952. "This change in western political life," wrote Lipset in reference to the "end of ideology," which supposedly accompanied the advent of abundance, "reflects the fact that the fundamental political problems of the industrial revolution have been solved." The idea that a progressive increase in aggregate income would lessen the harsh contrast between rich and poor is a doctrine as old as Daniel Webster. Postwar intellectuals understood that an obsession with gross national product had conservative implications, and many liberal Keynesians called for structural and social reforms. Yet it was hard to deny that the spectacle of affluence had replaced the specter of scarcity, making consumption the new opiate of the people. Werner Sombart's "melancholy" predictions at the turn of the century, made in his book *Why Is There No Socialism in the United States?* seemed to be coming true: "On the reefs of roast beef and apple pie socialistic utopias of every society are sent to their doom."[28]

Political Science: From Marx to Madison

The Old Left believed communism would resolve not only the problem of justice and equality but also the problem of power. The idea of a classless society implied that political power would be democratized as economic power was collectivized. But in Russia, the state, which Marx once called "the executive committee of the ruling class," failed to "wither away" even though the ruling classes had long been destroyed. The re-emergence of despotic power under Stalin puzzled the Old Left, and younger radicals, especially the Trotskyists, felt the need to go beyond orthodox Marxism to reconsider the elusive character of political power and to study the unanticipated phenomenon of postrevolutionary bureaucracy. The earlier writings of Italian elitist theorists like Vilfredo Pareto and Gaetano Mosca and the gloomy meditations of Max Weber haunted American intellectuals as they considered the prospect that oligarchy could emerge in all forms of modern society. Drawing upon these sources, James Burnham claimed to demonstrate the impossibility of democracy and the inevitability of a ruling class. The new ruling class, he argued, would be not the capitalists but the managerialists—the technicians and administrators who, by virtue of their essential skills, had assumed control over the means of production.[29]

To a large extent the deradicalization of intellectuals was a result of the impact of European totalitarianism upon American political thought. Stalinism was the mystery and the terror of the Old Left. In contrast to fascism, Stalinism could not be explained as a product of either monopoly capital or middle-class decadence. Unlike Hitler, Stalin was not the creator but the creation of a political system no one had foreseen. In the face of Soviet totalitarianism, American intellectuals began to reconsider the classical conservative argument against the monolithic state. Former radical students of politics like Martin Diamond and John P. Roche soon rejected Marx's theory of class conflict and rediscovered Madison's theory of factional conflict. The notion that democracy could be sustained only by a conflict among countervailing interest groups came to be known as liberal pluralism in the 1950's.

If Stalinism made former radicals fearful of centralization, fascism made them fearful of rampant egalitarianism. The paradox of fascism was that the more elitist and ruthless the regime became, the more popular it was in the eyes of the nation. As political scientists studied Mussolini's Italy and Hitler's Germany they began to sense that popular consent itself was inadequate to preserve democracy. Eventually a suspicion of mass movements in general developed, perhaps best expressed in Eric Hoffer's widely acclaimed *The True Believer* (1951) and in Walter Lippmann's *The Public Philosophy* (1955). A few political sociologists, like the former radical Lipset, even began to explore the forbidden subject of "working class authoritarianism." Having lost faith in the masses as the carriers of democratic values, social scientists in the 1950's could speak frankly of the positive benefits of public apathy. Mass involvement in politics and democratic participation in decision making became suspect to writers like Burnham, who believed that freedom must rest upon institutional foundations. Even more suspect was the role of theory in politics. The reaction against the revolutionary ideologies of communism and fascism became a reaction against

141

normative theory in general. The foundations of pluralism, Daniel Bell declared in explaining the failure of American socialism, rest on the "separation of ethics and politics." Those who tried to infuse politics with morality in order to transcend pluralism failed to heed Weber's dictum: "He who seeks the salvation of souls, his own as well as others, should not seek it along the avenue of politics."[30]

Theology: From Marx to Kierkegaard

After the Second World War, conscience politics did survive in one area—theology. Yet even here one finds a retreat from radicalism and a rejection of Marxism for the psychology of the soul. Former radicals like Reinhold Niebuhr and Will Herberg came to the conclusion that Marxism failed because it could not transcend the limitations of bourgeois culture. Marxism arose as a reaction to nineteenth-century liberalism, but it also absorbed liberalism's illusions about the rationality of man, the cult of technology, and the progressive nature of history. A millennialistic philosophy, Marxism placed the Kingdom of God in history and thereby falsely lifted the spiritual burden of freedom from the conscience of mankind. "History cannot solve our problems," wrote Herberg; "history is *itself* the problem." Above all, Marxism had rendered the Left oblivious to the ambiguities and corruptions of power. Private property is not the root of all evil; property is "not the cause but the instrument of human egotism," maintained Niebuhr. The human drive for power, as Hawthorne had pointed out a century earlier, is deeply rooted in the contradictory nature of man.[31]

The horrors of totalitarianism and the fallacies of liberalism drove theologians like Niebuhr and Herberg to develop a new theory of freedom that rejected Marx's world of social action for Kierkegaard's world of moral "inwardness." "Anxiety," declared Kierkegaard, "is the dizziness of freedom." In the inner dialogue of private conscience, freedom means anxiety because freedom requires making decisions in which all choices are finite, tragic, and guilt-ridden. In the teeth of liberal relativism and Marxist determinism, this existential definition of the authentically free man makes the individual the source of moral will and value judgment. Yet the tense strain of paradox and irony in Niebuhr's and Herberg's Christian existentialism undermined the

142

79 and 80   Reinhold Niebuhr *(left)* and Will Herberg *(right)*, two radical theologians who ultimately rejected Marxism.

utopian, millennialistic ethos of Marxism and deprived the Left of its worldly quest for paradise regained. Man had a moral duty to struggle for social justice but, fallen, could never escape the stain of sin and achieve self-transcendence. Significantly, the theologians' view of human nature led to the same political conclusions reached by the pluralists in social science. Both stressed the negative concept of freedom that called for restraints upon man's egotism. Thus the most democracy could achieve, given the dual nature of man, was balanced conflict and equilibrated power. "Man's capacity for justice makes democracy possible," observed Niebuhr; "but man's inclination to injustice makes democracy necessary." By tempering radical hopes with conservative fears, ex-Marxists like Niebuhr and Herberg gave America a theology of crisis that strengthened the fiber of American liberalism and strangled the millenialistic myths of American radicalism.[32]

Literature: From Marx to Melville

The controversy over proletarian realism in the thirties divided party Marxists from learned humanists and classicists and eventually demoralized the literary Left. Briefly, Marxists argued that all literature is a reflection of socioeconomic relations, and, since the class struggle is the core of human existence, the life of the proletariat is the proper

143

subject of art. Maintaining that most literature of the past represented an escape into bourgeois sentimentality or philosophical pessimism, the Marxists insisted that literature must lead to action rather than contemplation. Ignoring the fact that neither Marx nor Engels dared to lay down canons of literary theory, and ignoring Trotsky's observation that the proletariat was too "temporary and transient" to create its own culture, some American Marxists imposed formulas that reduced literature to a branch of sociology and made art into a crude class weapon. The result was a hack literature, mechanical in flow and metallic in flavor.

Most independent radical writers eventually rejected the monotony of proletarian realism. The tension between literary creativity and political dedication troubled learned *Partisan Review* critics like Phillips and Rahv, who refused to treat art as propaganda and to confine the literary imagination to political orthodoxy.[33] One result of the Old Left's repudiation of proletarian literature was a rediscovery of the value and integrity of American literature. In the 1920's writers had tended to look beyond provincial America for subject matter; and in the 1930's, Marxism reinforced the writers' conviction that the answer to America's social and cultural problems could be found only in Europe. The ideologies of Stalinism and fascism, however, discredited the appeal of European ideas, and the relativism of Marxism and Freudianism, which rendered absolute value judgments untenable, seemed to leave humanist intellectuals without solid principles on which to make a moral stand against Hitler. With the outbreak of the war, moreover, and with the influx of Europe's intellectual refugees, American writers came to feel that somehow their own fate and that of the rest of the world were inseparable from America's experience and destiny. No longer able to look to Europe as a cultural sanctuary or as a fount of political wisdom, literary critics now believed they could find a new, deeper strength and higher awareness in the classical works of Hawthorne, Whitman, Henry James, T. S. Eliot, and, above all, Melville—"the most plumbed and 'prophetic' of American writers," observed Louis Kronenberger. After the war the literary intellectuals' reconciliation with America reached a climax in 1952, when the *Partisan Review* published the symposium, "Our Country and Our Culture."

Actually the curious pattern of radical exhaustion and nationalistic celebration had been foreshadowed ten years earlier in Alfred Kazin's *On Native Grounds*, which marked the beginning of the Left's return home. The final chapter, "America! America!" opens with a remark by Abigail Adams to John Adams: "Do you know that European birds have not half the melody of ours?"[34]

American History: From Marx to Locke

The study of the American past followed somewhat the same pattern. American historians like Hacker also abandoned European Marxism in order to rediscover America. Unlike literary critics, however, historical scholars could scarcely return to the writings of classical American historians, none of whom, with the exception of Henry Adams, had envisioned the terrors of the twentieth century. Indeed, postwar historians even felt impelled to reject recent progressive historiography, which had depicted the American experience as a moral battleground between the forces of industrialism and agrarianism, capitalism and democracy, realism and idealism. Whereas literary intellectuals found in Melville and James a rich and complex vision of reality, historians found in Charles Beard and Vernon L. Parrington a simplistic and stilted theory of conflict. If economic conflict was the key to history, how did the United States survive a world depression and a world war with its institutions and values intact? After the war three prominent historians, Richard Hofstadter, Daniel J. Boorstin, and Louis Hartz, addressed themselves to this question of American uniqueness and exceptionalism. Significantly, all three had come of political age during the thirties; all had been influenced by Marxism, by what Boorstin called "the materialist interpretation of history." They never completely abandoned that perspective. For, although they departed from European Marxism in denying class conflict in America, they also departed from progressive historiography in denying moral conflict. What resulted was something of a Marxist description without a Marxist solution. Minimizing the role of democratic and ethical ideals, they still stressed the driving forces of economics, environment, and social structure.

Hofstadter discovered "a kind of mute organic consistency" in the ideologies of all major statesmen from Jefferson to Hoover, a philosophy

81-83   Historians Daniel Boorstin *(above left)*, Richard Hofstadter *(above right)*, and Louis Hartz *(below)*, who, though influenced by Marxist "materialist interpretations," later rejected the idea of class conflict for a consensus interpretation of the American past.

of economic individualism that bound Americans to the values of competitive capitalism and made America "a democracy of cupidity rather than a democracy of fraternity." In a critique similar to Marx's attack on nineteenth-century liberalism, Hofstadter observed that the American Constitution had dehumanized man by sanctifying property and by codifying a Hobbesian view of unchanging human nature. "Modern humanistic thinkers who seek for a means by which society may transcend eternal conflict and rigid adherence to property" would find no answer in the philosophy of the Founding Fathers.[35]

Where Hofstadter located America's political values in the repugnant "cupidity" of bourgeois liberalism, Boorstin located them in the resplendent spaciousness of the American environment. Since Americans believed that values arose not from mind but from nature, Boorstin found the American "genius" in the mindless activity of a Paul Bunyan rather than in the heightened consciousness of a William James, in the "unpredicted whisperings of environment" rather than in the theoretical and moral intellect. Louis Hartz also realized that the American political mind had little capacity for moral vision, but while Boorstin celebrated the discovery, Hartz, like Hofstadter, deplored it. In a brilliant analysis of the relationship between social structure and ideology, Hartz maintained that the absence of a feudal heritage in America led naturally to the development of middle-class, Lockian liberalism, which made the acquisition of property tantamount to the "pursuit of happiness." Because America did not experience a real social revolution in 1776, America was "born free" (Tocqueville's phrase). Lacking an *ancien régime* to resist radical change, America also lacked a mass socialist movement struggling *for* radical change. The absence of an entrenched, anti-industrial Right in America deprived the Left of an identifiable enemy against which a hostile class consciousness might have developed. Since there was neither a landed aristocracy to destroy nor a landless mob to denounce, liberalism absorbed America.[36]

The historiography of consensus and continuity that emerged in the 1950's is fraught with irony. So placid and homogenized did the image of the American past become that many historians began to argue whether there was anything to argue about. Moreover, the description of Americans as a homely people whose mental horizons had been bounded by common political attitudes and economic values began more and more to seem like the false consciousness of "one-dimensional man" that Herbert Marcuse popularized the following decade. Indeed, Boorstin and Marcuse could agree, albeit for different reasons, that Americans lacked a radical ideology and a theoretical vision enabling them to transcend the "given" values of capitalism. But the final irony is that Hartz himself anticipated a way out for radicals who could find no inspiration in a consensualized American past. More than any other historian, Hartz realized that America's "irrational Lockianism" had become "one of the most powerful absolutisms in the world," and he knew that America would be incapable of sympathizing with the need for radical change at home and revolutions abroad. "Can a people 'born equal' ever understand peoples elsewhere that have to become so? Can it ever understand itself?" Unlike most literary scholars and historians of the fifties, Hartz was one of the few writers who perceived that America's intellectual heritage could provide no answers to the troubling dilemmas of modern political life. "Instead of recapturing our past, we have got to transcend it . . . There is no going home again for America." In contrast to Boorstin, who was convinced that the outside world had nothing to teach America, Hartz maintained that "America must look to its contact with other nations to provide that spark of philosophy, that grain of relative insight that its own history has denied it." The New Left of the 1960's would scarcely be aware of how it had followed Hartz's advice when it found in the "third world" a flash of radical insight that the American past had denied it.[37]

Philosophy: From Marx to James

American historians could use a truncated Marxist mode of analysis to explain the "uniqueness" of America, but few intellectuals could accept the philosophical propositions upon which the entire structure of Marxist thought depends. The premises of historical materialism led to a battery of unresolved questions: To what extent do the ideas of human beings react upon the environment? Do changes in material circumstances affect real changes in mind? If man is governed by laws "independent of human will, consciousness, and intelligence," can individuals influence the course of history? These issues were thrashed out in learned journals like the *Marxist Quarterly* and *Modern Monthly*. Among philosophers, Sidney Hook established himself as the logician of the American Left with the publication of *Towards the Understanding of Karl Marx: A Revolutionary Interpretation* (1933). Here he tried to Americanize Marxism by demonstrating that the Marxist theory of knowledge as *praxis*—that is, proving ideas in social action—could be found in the "epistemological activism" of James and Dewey. Hook's erudite essays on Marxism, pondered by students and young radicals, were circulated "like the reports of the great theologians' disputes in the Middle Ages," recalled Lewis Feuer. "Copies of the *Symposium* and *Modern Monthly* articles were passed among impecunious undergraduate hands. Soon, however, a warning spread through the left-wing

84   Sidney Hook, logician of the Old Left in the 1930's, who became critical of many of its theoretical foundations.

grapevine: Hook is a revisionist."[38] Communists regarded the scrappy Hook as subversive because, aside from his political independence, he dared to question the mystique of dialectical materialism. The dialectic is the fountainhead of Marxist optimism. That all history is class conflict, that capitalism and socialism are absolute polar opposites precluding all other alternatives, and that revolution will negate all the existential contradictions in man's social life are convictions deeply rooted in the dialectic. Basically an illuminating concept of change involving the contradiction and reconciliation of a triadic thesis, antithesis, and synthesis, the dialectic became a vessel into which any idea could be poured. To Marxists the triad suggested feudalism, capitalism, and socialism; but to Christians it could mean the creation, the fall, and the redemption, and to Freudians, instinct, repression, and sublimation. All along, many academic philosophers had doubted the validity of the dialectic, and in 1940 three important books appeared that repudiated it as either religious myth, pseudologic, or even a Pythagorean allusion suggesting the insurgent power of a phallic symbol: Max Eastman's *Marxism is it Science,* Hook's *Reason, Social Myths and Democracy,* and Edmund Wilson's *To the Finland Station.* Three years later Hook went even further and challenged the whole Marxist 149 approach to historical understanding in *The Hero in History*. Maintaining that great "event-making" personalities like Lenin had decisively influenced the course of history, Hook returned to William James' classical protest against absolute determinism.

The crisis in philosophical Marxism resulted in large part from the inability of Marxists to predict the failure of the proletariat and the triumph of Hitler and Stalin. Instead of an experimental guide to action, Marxist philosophy now appeared an ironclad system of laws that gave intellectuals what James had once derided as the "sumptuosity of security." Some philosophers, like Hook and Roy Wood Sellars, salvaged from Marxism its brilliant epistemological insights and its materialist analysis of social change. Others abandoned Marxism completely for humanism or existentialism. What was curious about the discussion of Marxism in the late thirties and early forties was the absence of any mention of "alienation." The "God that failed" the Old Left was the cold, thundering prophet of scientific laws and historical doom. The Old Left was not aware of the younger Marx of the "Economic and Philosophic Manuscripts" (1844), where one finds the first conceptualization of alienation as rooted in the monotony of industrial work. It is in this document that the New Left of the 1960's found a vital ethical consciousness in Marxism. Henceforth Marx could no longer be treated simply as the demon of the dialectic. When Marxism emerged again in American radical thought it was not as a crude science of prediction but as a penetrating, humanist critique of the sickness of modern society.

PESSIMISM AND RELEVANCE
THE GULF BETWEEN

Between the Old Left of the 1930's and the New Left of the 1960's would lie a gulf of hostility. Younger students rejected the Marxist critique that older radicals tried to pass along. This generational denial was unfortunate. For the existentialism that some ex-Marxists espoused after the Second World War was not completely incompatible with radicalism, as Jean Paul Sartre would demonstrate; Burnham's theory of bureaucratic and technological power could be critically applied to the elitist structure of American society, as C. Wright Mills would demonstrate; and the Judeo-Christian sense of tragedy, which Niebuhr and Herberg rediscovered, could be elevated to a higher anguish of social guilt and political responsibility, as Michael Harrington would demonstrate in his writings and Martin Luther King in his actions. Ultimately, what discredited the Old Left and caused it to lose moral authority in the eyes of a younger generation was the cold war. After Stalinism and the Soviet occupation of eastern Europe, the Old Left became convinced that democratic freedom and one-party dictatorships are incompatible. After the experience of McCarthyism, an anticommunist hysteria that fed upon cold-war tensions, the waning Left lived in a constant fear of "witch hunts" and right-wing repression. Unable to believe in democratic revolution abroad and radical change at home, veteran Leftists could no longer sustain their vital spirit, their will to believe that existing reality can be negated and transformed, that ideals can be realized despite the dark record of historical experience.

A change of temper came over the radical intellectuals as they moved into the 1950's and out of politics, addressing themselves in *Partisan Review* to cultural criticism and the problem of mass society. Even in the politically conscious *Dissent,* writers felt deeply the loss of innocence and good hope. The simple faiths of former Trotskyists like Howe gave way to a feeling for the moral complexities of political action and the structural complexities of political power. Thus, when the nearly defunct Old Left saw familiar radical mythologies re-emerging in the 1960's, the only counsel it could impart was the counsel of failure. "Ours, a 'twice born' generation," wrote Daniel Bell, "finds its wisdom in pessimism, evil, tragedy, and despair. So we are both old and young before our time."[39] The New Left of the 1960's rejected the tragic mood of ambiguity and irony that hung over the collective memory of older radicals. The Old Left could only offer the lessons of experience, which to a subsequent generation must always seem like wisdom without power and knowledge without action. The cry that went up in the 1960's for "relevance" became a cry not for truth itself but for a truth that could be made politically useful. The Old Left could not respond to this demand. Having tasted power and having seen the future, the

151

"twice born" generation rejected both. Richard Hofstadter poignantly summed up the pathos of his generation of the thirties: "The war, the bomb, the death camps wrote finis to an era of human sensibility, and many writers of the recent past were immolated in the ashes, caught up like the people of Pompeii in the midst of life, some of them in curious postures of unconsummated rebellion."[40]

Notes

[1] Leon Trotsky, *The History of the Russian Revolution*, Vol. III, *The Triumph of the Soviets*, trans. Max Eastman (Ann Arbor: Univ. of Michigan Press, 1967), p. 174.

[2] Caroline Bird's phrase, quoted in Studs Terkel, *Hard Times: An Oral History of the Great Depression* (New York: Pantheon, 1970), p. 3.

[3] Edmund Wilson, "The Literary Consequences of the Crash," in *Shores of Light: A Literary Chronicle of the Twenties and Thirties* (New York: Farrar, 1952), pp. 498–99.

[4] F. Scott Fitzgerald, *The Crack-Up*, ed. Edmund Wilson (New York: New Directions, 1956), pp. 79-84.

[5] Lawson to Dos Passos, n.d., Dos Passos mss, Alderman Library, University of Virginia, Charlottesville, Va.; Granville Hicks, "Communism and the American Intellectuals," in *Whose Revolution?* ed. Irving D. Talmadge (New York: Howell, Soskin, 1941), p. 84.

[6] Sidney Hook, *Toward an Understanding of Karl Marx: A Revolutionary Interpretation* (New York: John Day, 1933); Louis Hacker, "The American Revolution," *Marxist Quarterly*, I (Jan.–Mar., 1937), 46-67; *id.*, "The American Civil War," *Marxist Quarterly*, I (Apr.–June, 1937), 191–213; Lewis Corey, "Veblen and Marxism," *Marxist Quarterly*, I (Jan.–Mar., 1937), 162–68.

[7] Aaron, *Writers on the Left*, p. 158.

[8] Irving Howe, "A Memoir of the Thirties," in *Steady Work: Essays in the Politics of Democratic Radicalism, 1953-1966* (New York: Harcourt, 1966), pp. 357–59.

[9] Floyd Dell, quoted in Freeman, *An American Testament*, p. 404; and in Aaron, pp. 217–18; Gold to Calverton, May 4, 1925, Calverton mss, New York Public Library.

[10] Georg Lukacs, *History and Class Consciousness: Studies in Marxist Dialectics*, trans. Rodney Livingstone (Cambridge, Mass.: M.I.T. Press, 1971), pp. 1–24; Arthur Koestler, *Arrow in the Blue* (New York: Macmillan, 1952), p. 272.

[11] Freeman, p. 663.

[12] Dos Passos's remark is in the important symposium, "Whither the American Writer," *Modern Quarterly*, VI (Summer, 1932), 11–12.

[13] Staughton Lynd, ed., "Personal Histories of the Early CIO," *Radical America*, V (May–June, 1971), 49–85; Theodore Draper, "Gastonia Revisited," *Social Research*, XXXVIII (Spring, 1971), 3–29; *id.*, "Communists and Miners, 1928–1933," *Dissent*, XIX (Spring, 1972), 371–92; see also John L. Shover, "The Communist Party and the Midwest Farm Crisis of 1933," *Journal of American History*, LI (Sept., 1964), 248–66.

[14] Dan T. Carter, *Scottsboro: A Tragedy of the American South* (Baton Rouge: Louisiana State Univ. Press, 1969), pp. 51–103; John P. Diggins, *Mussolini and Fascism: The View from America* (Princeton, N.J.: Princeton Univ. Press, 1972), pp. 306–12.

[15] Quoted in Hal Draper, "The Student Movement of the Thirties," in *As We Saw the Thirties*, ed. Rita Simon (Urbana: Univ. of Illinois Press, 1969), p. 156.

[16] *Ibid.*, p. 176.

[17] Nathan Glazer, *The Social Bases of American Communism* (New York: Harcourt, 1961).

[18] Theodore Draper, "The Ghost of Social Fascism," *Commentary*, XLVII (Feb., 1969), 29–42; Diggins, *Mussolini and Fascism*, pp. 213–20.

[19] Quoted in Irving Howe and Lewis Coser, *The American Communist Party: A Critical History* (New York: Praeger, 1957), p. 338.

[20] Upton Sinclair, quoted in Frank A. Warren, *Liberals and Communism: The "Red Decade" Revisited* (Bloomington: Indiana Univ. Press, 1966), p. 116.

[21] Hemingway to Dos Passos, 1938, Dos Passos mss.

[22] Lovestone, "The Moscow Trials in Historical Perspective," *Workers Age*, VI (Feb. 6, 1937), 3.

[23] Wilson, "American Critics, Left and Right," in *Shores of Light*, p. 643; Waldo Frank, *Chart for Rough Water* (New York: Doubleday, 1940), p. 43; Malcolm Cowley, "The Sense of Guilt," *The Kenyon Review*, CV (Spring, 1965), 265.

[24] Max Schactman, "Is Russia a Workers' State?" *The New International*, VI (Dec., 1940), 195–205.

[25] W. H. Auden, quoted in George Novack, "Radical Intellectuals in the 1930's," *International Socialist Review*, XXIX (Mar.–Apr., 1968), 33; Hicks, "Communism and the American Intellectuals," pp. 107–08.

[26] Karl Marx, *Das Kapital*, Vol. I (Chicago: Charles Kerr, 1906), p. 837.

[27] Lewis Corey, *The Crisis of the Middle Class* (New York: Covici, Friede, 1935); id., "American Class Relations," *The Marxist Quarterly*, (Apr.–June, 1937), 134–43; id., "The Middle Class," *Antioch Review*, V (Spring, 1945), 68–87; Max Lerner, *America as a Civilization* (New York: Simon & Schuster, 1957), pp. 465–540; Seymour Martin Lipset, *Political Man*, pp. 1-63.

[28] John Kenneth Galbraith, *American Capitalism: The Concept of Countervailing Power.* (Boston: Houghton Mifflin, 1952), p. 193; Lipset, p.442; Werner Sombart, quoted in Bell, *End of Ideology*, pp. 276–77.

[29] James Burnham, *The Managerial Revolution* (New York: John Day, 1941).

[30] Lipset, pp. 87–126; Max Weber, quoted in Bell, p. 275.

[31] Will Herberg, "From Marxism to Judaism," *Commentary*, III (Jan., 1947) 25–32; id., *Judaism and Modern Man* (New York: Farrar, 1951), p. 28; Reinhold Niebuhr, *The Children of Light and the Children of Darkness* (New York: Scribner, 1944), pp. 86–118.

[32] Herberg, *Judaism and Modern Man*, pp. 8–43; Niebuhr, *Children of Light*, p. xiii; for the influence of Niebuhr on American liberalism, see the essays by Kenneth Thompson, Arthur Schlesinger, Jr., and David Williams in Charles W. Kegley and Robert W. Bretall, *Reinhold Niebuhr: His Religious, Social, and Political Thought* (New York: Macmillan, 1956), pp. 126–75, 194–213.

[33] "The Situation in American Writing: Seven Questions," *Partisan Review*, VI (Summer, 1939), 25–51.

[34] Louis Kronenberger's remark is from the symposium "Our Country and Our Culture," an important intellectual document of the 1950's that ran in three issues of the *Partisan Review*, XIX (May–June, July–Aug., Sept.–Oct.), 282–326, 420–50, 562–97; Alfred Kazin, *On Native Grounds*, p. 485.

[35] Richard Hofstadter, *The American Political Tradition* (New York: Knopf, 1948), pp. viii, 16–17, *passim*.

[36] Daniel J. Boorstin, *The Genius of American Politics* (Chicago: Univ. of Chicago Press, 1953); Louis Hartz, *The Liberal Tradition in America* (New York: Harcourt, 1955); see also John P. Diggins, "Consciousness and Ideology in American History: The Burden of Daniel J. Boorstin," *American Historical Review*, LXXVI (Feb., 1971), 99–118.

[37] Hartz, *Liberal Tradition*, pp. 32, 309.

[38] Lewis S. Feuer, "From Ideology to Philosophy: Sidney Hook's Writings on Marxism," in *Sidney Hook and the Contemporary World: Essays on the Pragmatic Intelligence*, ed. Paul Kurtz (New York: John Day, 1968), p. 37.

[39] Bell, *End of Ideology*, p. 300.

[40] Richard Hofstadter, *The Progressive Historians* (New York: Knopf, 1968), p. 357.

154

The New Left 6

Communism? Who the hell knows from
Communism? We never lived through
Stalin. We read about it, but it doesn't af-
fect us emotionally. Our emotional reaction
to Communism is Fidel marching into
Havana in 1959.

Jerry Rubin

Nothing is clearer to a later generation than
the naivety of an earlier one, just as nothing
is clearer to the earlier one than the naivety
of the later.

Stephen Spender

In 1960, in Greensboro, North Carolina, four black students s pped
up to a segregated Woolworth's lunch counter and quietly asked to be
served. Three years later four black children died in the dynamiting
of the Sixteenth Street Baptist Church in Birmingham, Alabama. In
1961, Robert Moses, a northern student steeped in Camus, trekked alone
into the deepest and most violent parts of the South to register black
voters. Three years later the bodies of slain civil-rights workers James
Cheney, Andrew Goodman, and Michael Schwerner were found in an
earthen dam in Mississippi. Those were some of the unifying events
for a new generation whose demand for public morality was answered
with murder.

85 Antisegregationists picket a Woolworth's store in Raleigh, North Carolina, in 1960.

The radicalism of the 1960's was born in deed, not in doctrine. The action began in the South, America's moral looking-glass and embarrassing mirror image. The antisegregation protests soon spread to northern cities, where young whites and blacks engaged in peaceful sit-in demonstrations against job discrimination. The 1964 Berkeley Free Speech movement was a galvanizing experience after which the college campus would become the scene of bitter confrontations and escalating radical demands. As the 1960's unfolded, the New Left moved backwards into the 1930's. Starting with nonideological reformist goals, it would end by issuing heavily doctrinaire ultimatums. The Old Left began with a whoop of revolution and sank into a whimper of reconciliation—thanks to Russia; the New Left started in a spirit of moderation and ended calling for nothing less than revolution—thanks to America.

The New Left was one of the great political surprises of the mid-twentieth century. It arose suddenly, in the wake of the quiescent conformism of the politically silent generation of the fifties. Something of a historical mutation, its appearance defied the expectations of sociologists, who depicted American youths as "other-directed" personalities and the corporation men of the future. It defied opinion surveyors, who found students conservative and politically apathetic. And it defied the Old Left, which had declared America the graveyard of radicalism. In order to begin to understand the phenomenon of the New Left, or perhaps not to misunderstand it, it is necessary to discuss briefly three interrelated developments that provided its historical setting: the economic context of affluence and guilt, the political context of disillusionment and powerlessness, and the cultural context of alienation and anxiety.

FROM ALIENATION TO ACTIVISM

Young radicals of the sixties were mainly the children of parents who had grown up in the thirties and forties. Rushed into adulthood after having survived the privations of depression and war, their parents embarked upon a frenzy of spending and building. Systematically they bulldozed the American landscape, replacing it with shopping centers and ticky-tacky housing developments until the monotony of the environment began to resemble the drab uniformity of a Second World War army camp. While showering the children with the good things in life that had been denied them, the parents were too busy getting ahead to conceive life in any deeper terms than those of economic security and material comfort. Frozen at the level of material existence, American society became an antiseptic wasteland of stucco and plastic; echoing Henry Miller, the Beat poets of the fifties called it "an air-conditioned nightmare."

Jaded by affluence, estranged from parents who so valued this affluence, young radicals began to sense that their midde-class alienation had something in common with lower-class exploitation. The key social document for the early sixties was Michael Harrington's *The Other America* (1963). Here high-school seniors and college freshmen first read about the desperate "invisible poor," who had been hidden from America by a mental wall of suburban content. The discovery of the existence of poverty and racism in the ghettos of the North as well as the South brought forth what Jack Newfield described as "a kind of mass vomit against the hypocrisy of segregation." At first middle-class

86 Typical uniformity
and regimentation in a
huge suburban housing
subdivision in San Le-
andro, California.

youths, nurtured by their parents' part-time liberalism, found some
hope for change in the Kennedy administration. But as the New Frontier
turned out to be more style than substance, young activists thirsted all
the more for a new politics of personal witness and moral confrontation.
According to Tom Hayden, those who worked on voter registration in
the South experienced "schizoid or ambivalent feelings" toward the
White House, which "might" support their efforts only "when push
came to shove." When President Kennedy was assassinated, on November 22, 1963, ambivalence turned to anguish as young people felt more
politically alone than ever. "For me this one act," a student told his
professor, "has made all other acts irrelevant and trivial; it has dis-

placed time with paranoia, good with evil, relative simplicity with incomprehensibility, and an ideal with dirt."[1]

The same sense of personal loss and political distrust grew also out of the diplomatic developments of the sixties. The young, who had inherited the atomic bomb as a child inherits an incurable disease, originally looked to Kennedy as an idealist without illusions. The new President refrained from attacking neutralism, established the Peace Corps as a means of helping underdeveloped countries, and allowed his ambassador to the United Nations, the urbane Adlai Stevenson, to speak of the need to "make the world safe for diversity." But any hope that there would be a re-examination of America's cold-war policies was soon shattered by the Bay of Pigs invasion (April, 1961), which indicated to many that the President had rejected the old strategy of the threat of massive nuclear retaliation only to adopt the covert strategy of counter-insurgency. Young radicals, now beginning to identify with the political and economic destiny of the "third world," embraced Fidel Castro as the embodiment of a "new humanist socialism" while attacking the faceless, bureaucratic "socialism" of eastern Europe.[2]

With Kennedy's death, American militarism, always latent in his administration, grew malignant. Thereafter America's increasing involvement in the Vietnam war dramatized to young anti-war dissenters

87   Activist Tom Hayden, once leader of the SDS, at the time of his trial (with seven others) for conspiracy to riot at the 1968 Democratic National Convention in Chicago.

the powerlessness of idealism. Hopes for an end of the interminable war were aroused in the 1968 democratic primaries, when Senators Eugene McCarthy and Robert Kennedy challenged President Lyndon Johnson's renomination. But McCarthy's following was confined to young white liberals; and an assassin's bullet tragically cut short the promising career of the young Kennedy, the only major candidate who appealed to the blacks and Chicanos as well as some white radicals—perhaps the only one who might have been able to put together a "rainbow coalition." As Kennedy's body lay in state in St. Patrick's Cathedral, activist Tom Hayden was seen sitting in the rear, crying quietly and holding in his hand a guerrilla beret given to him by Fidel Castro.

The culture of the young, especially their rock and folk music, reflected their growing mood of frustration and powerlessness. Contrapuntal notes of joy and sadness, love and loneliness, fantasy and dread reverberated in the lyrics of the Beatles, Jimi Hendrix, the Jefferson Airplane, and Bob Dylan. The optimistic call for revolt was often accompanied by a fatalistic sense of political impotence and an acute conviction that filial love was a snare and the "American Dream" a fraud. Hence the Jefferson Airplane:

> War's a good business, so give your son . . .
> And I'd rather have my country die for me . . .
> Sell your mother for a Hershey bar
> Grow up looking like a car.*

The demon of technology also emerged as a rock theme. The young felt that a technolological culture denied man's autonomy and the reality of values like beauty and love, mystery and imagination. And behind the cult of the machine lurked the imminence of holocaust, as the poet Dylan prophesies:

> This wheel's on fire
> Rolling down the road
> Just notify my next of kin
> This wheel shall explode.†

*From REJOYCE by Grace Slick. © 1968 by Icebag Corp. All rights reserved. Reprinted by permission.
†From THIS WHEEL'S ON FIRE, words by Bob Dylan. © 1967 Dwarf Music. Reprinted by permission.

The cultural alienation of the young also signified an increasing rejection of the values of the industrial way of life: work, duty, rationality, and mastery of the environment. More and more middle-class youths began to turn against these Protestant values in order to recapture nature and feeling. The romantic pastoralism was most pronounced in the hippie phenomenon. The children of this new ethereal culture appeared to have moved beyond not only capitalism but materialism itself. Their communal life style suggested a sustained willingness to share all one's possessions so that the body might be dispossessed and the "soul" freed. In search of new, nonrational sources of wisdom, hippies turned to intuition, telepathy, and the occult; and in their quest for moral purification and self-expression they displayed a remarkable indifference to organizational failure. Their only fear was the institutionalized boredom of their parents—what the earlier Puritans used to call deadness of heart. Some hippies took up Zen, Lao-tzu, and tantric Yoga, desiring, in the spirit of Thoreau, to transcend physical reality; others became disciples of Wilhelm Reich and Norman O. Brown, desiring, in the spirit of Whitman, to immerse themselves in the pleasures of the body and embrace the holiness of sin. Toward the end of the 1960's America witnessed a series of Dionysiac folk-rock festivals—huge, organized "happenings" celebrating passion, experience, and fulfillment, instead of the old western culture of reason, knowledge, and achievement. "Every period which abounded in folk songs has, by the same token, been deeply stirred by Dionysiac currents," wrote Nietzsche a century ago.[3]

The emergence of what Theodore Roszak called a "counter culture" accounted for the unusual degree of personalism and humanism in the early New Left. Young radicals shared the hippies' desire to restore warmth to human relationships, to translate social problems into dialogues of conscience that would lead to moral action. Originally a psychoethical rather than a doctrinal movement, the New Left also felt the need to achieve "authenticity." Yet, before long, the hippies' antipolitics of solipsism and ecstasy became unacceptable to many New Left activists. For one thing, the old epistemological problem divided the hippies from the activists in much the same way it had divided the nineteenth-century transcendentalists from the abolitionists: If feeling 161

88 Part of the throng at the huge folk-rock festival in Woodstock, New York, in 1970, an instance of changes in life style wrought by the "counterculture." Many participants believed themselves to be making a "new nation."

determines reality, as the hippies maintained, then the poor and oppressed were merely those who felt poor and oppressed. Salvation lay not in changing conditions but in changing perceptions—and the door to perception was not politics but psychedelia ("Imagination is Revolution!"). Moreover, when the hippies spoke of peace and love they were talking about an ethic of passivity, a creative quietism that seemed dangerously innocent to experienced activists. Hippies may not have been going through the "technological obsolescence of masculinity," as Leslie Fiedler charged when he described the tight pants and long hair of males who saw themselves as "more seduced than seducing," but no doubt there was a tenderness to their life style that transformed the traditionally aggressive male into a political cipher. Power grows out of the barrel of a gun, the New Left was convinced, not from the bud of a flower.[4]

Antecedent Lefts: Differences and Similarities

Despite these differences, the New Left and the hippies were alienated allies. The same could not be said for the New Left and the Old Left.

162

89 Members of a New Mexico commune in meditation, one expression of the alienation of the young not politicized by the New Left.

The New Left's main charge against the old radicals was the *"trahison des clercs,"* the intellectual cop-out of ex-Troyskyists like Irving Howe and Dwight Macdonald, who supposedly compromised their Leftism by their anticommunism, and of leaders like Michael Harrington and Bayard Rustin, older labor movement radicals who chose to work through the system. Advocating coalition politics and reformist programs, the Old Left seemed to young radicals to have committed the sins of their fathers by becoming "establishment liberals."[5]

But the real difference between the two generations of radicals is more a matter of context than tactics. The historic context of the Old Left was the abundance of poverty, that of the New Left the poverty of abundance. The Depression led older radicals to believe that history would do for them what they could not do for themselves. Assuming that the masses would be radicalized as America went from bad to worse, they could find reassurance in the Trotskyist adage, "the worse the better." The children of affluence, however, confronted the other side of the proposition, and thus for them a change of consciousness had to precede, or at least accompany, a change of conditions. Their hope was that a socialist consciousness would develop as the victims of society liberated themselves through autonomous community action. The Old Left, educated on the realistic determinism of Marx and Lenin, remained skeptical of the noble dream that participatory democracy would engage the needs and interests of impoverished minority groups. The New Left, brought up on the psychological optimism of neo-Freudians like Eric Fromm and the communitarian ideals of progressive educationists, enjoyed endless visions of human possibility.

"As for old socialists," wrote the young novelist Jeremy Larner, "their limitations as people seem disastrous, and frustrate me insofar as they are my own. They appear to be tedious, tired of themselves, full of self-hate, and chained to an idealism so abstract that it precludes all love of life." The New Left claimed to be chained neither to doctrine nor to history. "The old Marxist Left was intensely ideological," stated the young organizer Clark Kissinger. "They could rattle off the cause of *any* war as capitalism, imperialism, fight for free markets: one two three. We are characterized primarily by skepticism. Not having all the answers, we don't pretend to." The New Left relied "more on feel than theory," explained Hayden. From the perspective of this new antinomianism, the unpardonable sin of the Old Left was less the inadequacy of its formal ideology than its loss of passion. "When they proclaim the end of ideology," stated Kissinger, "it's like an old man proclaiming the end of sex. Because he doesn't feel it anymore, he thinks it has disappeared." Yet if the young radicals could not tolerate the veteran's dried-up dogmatism, neither could the latter comprehend the youth's renascent mysticism, which seemed more symptomatic of a religious revival than a social revolution. "We went in for Talmudic exegesis," stated Fiedler to an audience of students, "you go in for holy rolling."6

In spirit, the New Left was originally closer to the 1913 rebels than to the Marxists of the thirties. For one thing, both generations saw themselves as self-conscious youth movements. Bourne's description of youth as the "rich rush and flood of energy" and his attacks on the "medievalism" of college education had their echo in the New Left's quest for original innocence and in its attacks on the "multiversity." Reed's and Dell's reflections on "Life at Thirty" indicated that the New Left was not the first generation to become obsessed with that age as the point at which self-trust turns to doubt. And Walter Weyl, in his postmortem on the "tired radicals" of the First World War, perceived that the Left's greatest enemy was age itself, a biological fact that has haunted both generations: "Adolescence is the true day of revolt, the day when obscure forces, as mysterious as growth, push us, trembling out of our narrow lives into the wide throbbing life beyond self."7

In its élan and anarchist bravado the New Left also resembled the Lyrical rebels. The parallel was particularly apparent with respect to the yippies, whose calculated strategy of sensation and shock seemed less designed to take power than to liquidate it by laughter. The impish antics of Reed and Dell, whose outlandish behavior offended party socialists, were carried on by Abbie Hoffman and Jerry Rubin, who believed that "confusion is mightier than the sword," that ideology was the "brain disease" of the Left, and that a "Be In" was a prelude to revolution. Women's rights, which was in the forefront of the New Left, had also been a passionate concern of the Lyrical rebels. Max and Crystal Eastman championed female suffrage and the emancipation of

165

90   Nudism in the theater—the cast of *Hair*—another reflection of "counterculture" influence.

the housewife from the drudgery of domesticity; and Emma Goldman's demand for complete sexual parity made her one of the founding sisters of the women's liberation movement. As for the sexual revolution itself, doubtless the New Left went much further. Dell and Eastman would have been bewildered by those youths of the 1960's who saw Freud as an oppressor of women ("Freud is a fink"), an aphrodisiac as the answer to alienation, and the orgasm of the body as the proper oblivion of the mind. The Lyrical Left had to struggle seriously against government censorship and the moral repression of society. The dilemma of the New Left was that government and society had become so permissive about sex that it found itself in a vacuum of nonresistance. Eventually, the underground culture had to escalate the flaunting of eroticism, from sex to nudity and ultimately to pornography, hoping to meet opposition so that it could expose American society as sick and repressed. But as the popular success of the musical *Hair* indicated, the American middle class was not outraged but titillated by private pleasures made public. Although the counterculture continued to believe that nakedness would liberate the mind from its "ego-defenses," the New Left wanted to make the revolution with its working clothes on.[8]

Cultural differences aside, the New Left almost echoed the Old Left in political rhetoric. Comparing the *New Masses* and *Modern Monthly*

166

of the 1930's with *Ramparts* and *Liberation* of the 1960's, one finds the same view of America as a "corporate state" bent on imperialistic war, the same equation of liberalism and fascism, and the same attack on the liberal Center in order to "shorten the birth pangs of history." Nor did the New Left disabuse itself of the older Stalinist cult of personality. The adulation of Chairman Mao allowed young radicals to dismiss the terrorism of the Red Guard with the same naiveté as older radicals had shown in dismissing the Moscow trials. The will to mythologize also remained characteristic. Despite Castro's courageous admission that Cuba had failed to advance workers' self-management through non-material incentives, the New Left still looked to Cuba's *campesinos* as models of participatory democracy, just as the Old Left once looked to Russia's collectives as models of grassroots democracy. Finally, although the New Left started out as an open, democratic, and nonideological movement, it became the opposite; by the end of the 1960's much of the

91 Mao Tse-tung, Chinese revolutionary leader and a focus of adulation by the PLP.

92 Cuba's Fidel Castro, leader of its revolution, esteemed by many of the New Left.

New Left had reverted to the stale clichés of economic Marxism, succumbed to the curse of sectarianism, and, like the Old Left, found itself in desperate isolation.

FROM PORT HURON TO PEKING

The Civil-Rights Movement

The Old Left died when communist Russia failed to fulfill its prophecies; the New Left was born when democratic America failed to keep its promises. The first stirrings of the postwar Left originated in the civil-rights movement. Led by respectable, middle-class black students, the southern antisegregation campaign was basically a moral protest entirely within the spirit of the law. For a century the South had been able to circumvent the Fourteenth and Fifteenth Amendments, which guaranteed voting rights and equal protection of the law to black Americans; and for almost a decade the South managed to sabotage the 1954 Supreme Court decision that ordered the immediate desegregation

168

of public schools. Thus, when the protests began in the South there was no call for social revolution. The tactics of civil disobedience and passive resistance reflected the Christian principles of love and justice, values that had lived on in a land where the black Baptist Church had instilled an ethic of stoic suffering. Visiting Amite, Mississippi, Jack Newfield observed that "a meeting in a broken-down shack called a church approaches Gandhian *agape* with the singing of religious hymns and the preachments of love thy neighbor." White students who risked their lives as Freedom Riders in 1961, and those who participated in the 1964 Mississippi Summer Project, discovered in the deep South "simple people living lives of relative peace, love, honor, courage, and humor." Their crusade became a "back-to-the-people" movement in which youths could struggle in interracial solidarity to overcome their isolated existence. "We seek a community," said one activist, "in which man can realize the full meaning of the self which demands open relationships with others."9

Students for a Democratic Society

The same quest for intimate community and selfhood inspired students in the North who were outraged by the cossack-like police charge against the Birmingham civil-rights demonstrators in late spring 1963. The northern movement first organized around the Students for a Democratic Society, which grew from a few dozen activists in 1962 to about 8000 core members at its height in 1968, when it also had 50,000 to 75,000 students casually affiliated through hundreds of campus chapters. More than any other organization, SDS shaped the tone and spirit of the early New Left. Generally from secure, upper-middle-class white families, SDS members included gifted graduate students and sophomore dropouts, Christian pacifists and militant confrontationists, weekend potheads and midnight mystics. Its "Port Huron Statement," drawn up in 1962, was the first manifesto in the history of the American Left to focus primarily on the problem of ethical existence. Here values like "fraternity," "honesty," and "love" were invoked to overcome the "estrangement" of modern man. Declaring that "our work is guided by the sense that we may be the last generation in the experiment with living," SDS attacked the deterrence theory of the cold

169

93   The 1963 Civil Rights Demonstration in Washington, D.C. The size was estimated at over 200,000 people.

war, the welfare state, the military-industrial complex, and the public's "crust of apathy." In 1963 SDS issued a second manifesto, "America and the New Era," criticizing the Kennedy administration as a "corporate liberal" political elite. SDS, it must be noted, also applied the same criticisms to the undemocratic structure of world communist parties, and it rejected what C. Wright Mills aptly called the "labor metaphysic"—the illusion that the working class would fulfill its Marxist-conferred mission of transforming capitalism into socialism. Instead of a workers' revolt, SDS called for a "democracy of individual participation" in which all people would share in the social decisions determining the quality of their lives. With the ethic of "participation" elevated to a political mystique, and with a small grant of $5,000 from the United Auto Workers, SDS set up the Economic Research and Action Project to organize the ghetto poor and develop neighborhood programs.

Progressive Labor Party

Compared to the vague, existential humanism of SDS, the doctrines of the Progressive Labor Party were depressingly familiar. PL was formed in 1962, when it broke with the CP and sided with the Red

94   Young marchers in the 1971 "Moratorium Day" rally against the war in Vietnam carry portraits of New and Old Left heroes.

Chinese during the Sino-Soviet rift. Maoist in inspiration, Leninist in organization, PL opposed the emotional anarchy and spontaneity of SDS. It subscribed to violence, believed armed struggle probable, cited Marxist-Leninist doctrine as gospel, and dredged up old terms like "exploitation" as the last word in social analysis. Intellectually PL was a throwback to the worst aspects of the Old Left. Offended by hippie sensuality, uptight about drugs, critical of counter-cultural heroes like Bob Dylan and Allen Ginsberg, PL seemed a parody of the grim radicalism that characterized the worst aspects of the Old Left.

Offshoots of the Old

Two other important organizations of the early New Left were the Young Socialist Alliance and the DuBois Clubs of America. The former represented the Trotskyist youth branch of the old Socialist Workers Party. The Trotskyists, keeping the faith of their namesake, continued to insist that only the working class could carry on the struggle against Soviet bureaucracy as well as American capitalism. Although numbering only a few hundred members at its birth, YSA picked up support in the late sixties. The DuBois Clubs defied all generalizations about generational revolt, for they were started by the children of former communists. Organized in 1964, the DuBois Clubs had roughly 1000 members concentrated in Berkeley, San Francisco, and New York. Like the post-Stalinist and conservative CP, the young communists advocated working with labor unions and supporting, when necessary, the liberal wing of the Democratic Party. In contrast to SDS, DuBois members believed in the enduring viability of Marxist theory; but in contrast to the Maoist fanaticism of PL, they feared the threat of a new McCarthyism and the possibility of native fascism more than they hated American liberalism.

Originally, SDS believed in the miracle of community organization, PL in the might of violent revolutionary struggle, YSA in the mystique of proletarian consciousness, and the DuBois Clubs in the method of coalition politics. Not surprisingly, SDS regarded PL as dangerously adventuristic, while the latter accused the former of "bourgeois romanticism": YSA criticized DuBois members for betraying the working class, and they in turn suspected young Trotskyists of ideological paranoia. Beyond the familiar polemics, the history of the Left in the sixties is the story of the demise of SDS and the rising influence of PL.

Two developments accounted for this shift from participatory socialism to revolutionary Maoism. First of all, the Vietnam war undermined SDS's argument that it was possible to work within the system. SDS was slow to realize the mounting hostility to the war. Concentrating on slum neighborhood projects, SDSers felt that the war was not directly related to the lives of the poor. SDS took an active part in draft resistance and campus confrontations with military recruiters and Dow Chemical Company (manufacturers of napalm), and it helped organize the 1965 March on Washington against the Vietnam war. But it was PL, invoking Lenin's First World War thesis on mobilizing the masses against capitalism and turning a national war into a class war, that could claim to have the "correct analysis" of the crisis. As more and more radicals came to regard Vietnam as a war of imperialistic aggression, PL's classical Marxism appeared to offer a solution.

Black Militants

Moreover, the growing militancy in the black civil-rights movement meant the Left could no longer be the exclusive province of middle-class whites. In 1964 Stokely Carmichael emerged in a fury of eloquent black rage, determined to liberate his people from internal "colonialism." That summer the Mississippi Freedom Democratic Party challenged the Democratic convention for representation on the all-white Mississippi delegation. After long, bitter negotiations, MFDP was granted two token seats, and militants came away convinced more than ever that "black power" was more important than civil rights. At first the black-power movement, possibly emboldened by the riots in Watts in 1965 and in Newark in 1967, repudiated its white supporters. During the 1967 Chicago convention of the National Conference for a New Politics—organized to promote the black leader Dr. Martin Luther King and the white antiwar spokesman Dr. Benjamin Spock on a presidential ticket—African-robed black radicals dictated inordinate demands on voting rights, seating arrangements, and resolutions, humiliating white participants, who groaned of "flagellating our white conscience" and of being "castrated." The following year, after the   173

95 Eldridge Cleaver (in short-sleeved *dashiki*) and Bobby Seale, Black Panther leaders at a news conference in 1969. Next to Seale is H. Rap Brown, the revolutionary agitator who went underground after the Newark riots.

tragic assassination of Dr. King, the Black Panthers emerged as the leading force of Afro-American militancy.[10]

The Black Panther Party had been formed in Oakland, California, in 1966 by Huey Newton and Bobby Seale. Originally the Panthers seemed just another small band of black nationalists, although better known than most because of their armed neighborhood patrols. Then Panther chapters sprung up in the ghettos of a dozen large cities, and their membership rose to about 5000 in 1968. At the same time the Panthers broadened their ideology. Inspired by third-world illuminati like Franz Fanon, Che Guevara, Ho Chi Minh, and Mao Tse-tung, the Panthers adopted a "Marxist-Leninist" amalgam that succeeded in combining nationalism with socialism, preaching self-determination along with class struggle. Unlike other black nationalist groups, the Panthers became convinced that a social revolution against racism and capitalism could be made only by a coalition of whites and blacks. Accordingly, they entered an alliance with the white-based Peace and Freedom Party, which ran the black writer Eldridge Cleaver for president in the 1968 election. Some white radical groups welcomed this ideological turn, but SDS could not accept the Panthers' claim that

174

RETALIATION TO CRIME: REVOLUTIONARY VIOLENCE
RÉPONSE AU CRIME: LA VIOLENCE RÉVOLUTIONNAIRE
RESPUESTA AL ASESINATO: VIOLENCIA REVOLUCIONARIA
الى العنف الثوري !

96   A Cuban poster celebrates "Black Power" in mutual admiration. From *The Art of Revolution: Castro's Cuba. 1959–70* by Susan Sontag and Dugald Stermer. Copyright 1971. Used with permission of McGraw-Hill Book Company.

they alone constituted the vanguard of the revolution. In July 1969, at a National Conference for a United Front Against Fascism in Oakland, Seale warned "those little bourgeois, snooty nose . . . SDS's" that if anyone "gets out of order" they can expect "disciplinary actions from the Black Panther Party."[11]

By 1970 the New Left was in disarray. Pressured on one side by Panther *machismo* and embarrassed on the other by yippie freakout, it could no longer sustain an impelling vision or offer a viable program of action. Without a unified, broad-based organization, without a leader who could inspire more than a small band of faithful adherents, the New Left remained what it always had been—a mood in search of a movement.

DECLINE WITH INFLUENCE

The decline of the New Left may be attributed to at least four factors, two of which, in particular, had been common to the experience of preceding Lefts in America.

The Agency of Change

The central dilemma that has faced all three Lefts in twentieth-century America was the inability to find a social force that would adopt a commitment of active opposition to the existing order. SDS originally hoped that at least some sections of the labor movement could be radicalized. But the American worker proved indifferent to the New Left and hostile to its libertarian life style. Spurned by trade unionists, young radicals later flirted with the idea of a "new working class" emerging among the frustrated, increasingly displaced technological intelligentsia. But under pressure from dogmatic Marxists who scorned this new outlook as "petit bourgeois revisionism," SDS dropped the notion of a white-collar working class. What remained for the non-communist Left were those groups that originally aroused the sympathy of young activists, the poor and the oppressed minorities, supposedly the last remnant of uncoopted virtue in America. Out of a population of 205 million, there were about 25 million "poor" in the United States. According to the 1970 census, this category included about 34 percent of the black people and about 10 percent of the white, roughly 7.5 million blacks out of a population of 23 million, and 16 million whites out of 168 million. The remaining poor were Puerto Ricans and Mexican-Americans—1.5 million and 500,000, respectively—and Indians and others. In the radical sense of the term, the poor scarcely constituted a solidified "social class" of the racially oppressed, since one-third of the nonwhite families in America had an income of more than $8,000 per year. Even more serious, since the poor of all colors represented a small minority (about 13 percent of the total population), it was no longer possible, as it was in the nineteenth century of Debs and Marx, to claim that the oppressed had on their side the power of numbers.[12]

In the beginning, the New Left was not blind to these realities. The original strategies of participatory democracy, community action, and self-determination implied that radical change had to be generated from among small minorities. Nevertheless, the strategy was unrealistic from the start. Establishing health clinics, garbage collection, and nursery schools were noble efforts that helped mitigate the suffering of the poor but did little to affect real social change. Community control could offer only control over poverty itself. Participatory democracy was the naive ideal of a generation that had been reared to believe that good will and "togetherness" could bring instant change. Innocent of the realities of power and the slow pace of historical change, lacking personal experience with the psychology of poverty, young radicals were unable to cope with setbacks and defeats.

The Vietnam War

The New Left shifted from domestic to international issues in February 1965, when the Johnson administration began systematic bombing of North Vietnam. Opposition to the war was first expressed in petitions, peaceful marches, and campus forums. By spring 1967, the antiwar movement assumed a new militant posture. Demonstrations now became massive, with participation by as many as 400,000 people (the April 1967 "mobilization" in New York and San Francisco); organized draft resistance penetrated several military camps, where servicemen risked being tried for mutiny by publicly protesting the war; and dozens of campuses exploded in a spasm of violent protests over issues like

97 Part of a 1971 anti-Vietnam war demonstration in San Francisco, one of several held nationwide on the same day.

98   Demonstration at Kent State University in Ohio at which four students were shot to death by National Guardsmen.

ROTC and on-campus military recruiting and classified war research. Yet the New Left could never successfully organize the discontent that the war had spawned. Even more serious, after accurately predicting the inevitable expansion of the war, the New Left found itself powerless to prevent what it had predicted. The moment of truth came in May 1970, when President Nixon announced his decision to invade Cambodia. America reeled in a torrent of student protest as white puffs of tear gas rose across the sky of campuses throughout the country. Students succeeded in closing down or impairing the operations of about 425 colleges, but at a tragic price. In New York City "hard hat" construction workers waded into a crowd of student demonstrators while police looked the other way; at Kent State in Ohio, four students were fatally shot by national guardsmen. Some revolutionists tried to escalate the confrontation on the campuses, but by the time the smoke had cleared,   179 a widespread revulsion against violence had developed. Many students who had been quickly radicalized by the events decided to go off campus in an attempt to "communicate" with middle America, to explain their opposition to the war, to organize support for peace candidates, and to take "the long walk through existing institutions." The following year, when the 1971 May Day mobilization was held, the antiwar movement belonged more to students and the public in general than to the New Left. "Peace has become respectable," shouted Jerry Rubin in disgust.[13]

Repression

Confrontation politics worked well on the campus, where the New Left could force professors who identified with their antiwar goals to capitulate to ever-increasing demands and could effectively exploit the television medium to create the impression that it spoke for the majority of students. Outside the sanctuary of the campus, however, confrontation brought a backlash of repression. The nasty awakening

99   A Chicago policeman sprays demonstrators at the 1968 Democratic National Convention with Mace, a disabling riot-control compound.

100 A demonstrator and a National Guardsman in a staring match at the 1968 Chicago demonstration. As the photograph suggests, the "gap" was not only between generations.

came during the Democratic convention of June 1968, when the Left announced its intention to disrupt the proceedings, only to discover the brute power of Mayor Richard Daley's police force. Every opinion poll indicated that the substantial majority of the public supported Daley's inept, merciless treatment of the screaming demonstrators. Presidential candidate Richard Nixon, playing to the fears of middle America, made "law and order" the catchword of his campaign. With the crackdown on campus disorders, the increase in school expulsions, and the stepped-up war on drugs, the era of tolerance had ended.

No longer could the Left organize demonstrations without fear of indictment, mount the barricades without fear of the National Guard, 181

101 The National Guard disperses demonstrators with tear gas at the Berkeley, California "shut-it-down" strike.

abuse the symbols of America without fear of the hard hats. There was no doubt now that the government would have the full support of the majority of the citizenry should it resort to even the severest measures to suppress the Left. Significantly, the Black Panthers, the most harassed of all radical groups, were among the first to realize that the game of confrontation politics was over. In May 1970, when a rally was held in New Haven in support of the imprisoned Bobby Seale, the Panthers tried to tone down the demonstration for fear of government reprisal. After the Cambodia crisis, American campuses lapsed into a strange mood of quiet frustration and fatigue—what Yale President Kingman Brewster called an "eerie tranquility."

Factionalism and Suicidal Extremism

Like all Lefts, the New Left acted out the dismal pattern of faction and fission. Even the tightly organized Panthers divided into rival sects that accused each other of being police informers or male chauvinists.

But the dissolution of SDS had repercussions for the entire Left. In the early 1960's PL had set up the May 2nd Movement in an attempt to compete with the more popular and more youthful SDS. But in 1965 PL dissolved this branch and entered SDS. Once inside, PL charged SDS with student elitism and middle-class condescension toward American workers. As a result, SDS split wide open at its 1969 convention, with a majority going over to the Maoist PL. At the same time radicals began to look beyond the campus and the ghetto in order to end the isolation of the academic intelligentsia from the mass of workers. The attempt to forge a "worker-student alliance" (WSA) was prompted in part by the dramatic May 1968 uprising of what radicals saw as a coalition of French industrial workers and Parisian students. The newly formed WSA accepted PL's thesis that only the working class possessed the leverage crucial to achieving radical change in America. But the students' attempt to infiltrate the factories and support workers' causes met with little success. In November 1970, 750 members of the now decimated SDS turned out in Detroit to demonstrate before the General Motors Building and join the automotive strikers. According to reporters, not a factory worker was in sight.[14]

Meanwhile another faction had been developing within SDS—the Revolutionary Youth Movement. Skeptical of the potential of students and workers alike, RYM maintained that it was a mistake to try to make a revolution in one country when in reality it had already begun in Vietnam, Cuba, and the rest of the third world. The role of the Left was thus to align itself with the international revolution abroad by engaging in irregular warfare behind enemy lines, thereby undermining the overextended power of America's imperialistic war machine. Out of this new strategy came the Weathermen, an underground guerilla cadre who believed that the core of the "Red Army" could be built in the streets of America through the symbolic power of violence. This American version of the nineteenth-century Russian *Narodniki* (terrorists) staged its first encounter in Chicago in October 1969. Dressed in helmets and blue denims, trained in karate, the Weathermen went on a three-day "trashing" rampage until the police arrested 290 of its 300 members. While radical critics accused the Weathermen of suicidal "Custerism," several fugitives escaped to New York and planned to intensify their campaign through the use of well-placed bombs. In March 1970, three members accidentally killed themselves while preparing explosives in a Greenwich Village townhouse.

The mangled bodies found in a basement in Greenwich Village—spiritual home of the first Lyrical rebels—dramatized the tragic desperation and exhaustion of the New Left. During the early civil-rights movement radical youths tried to work through the liberal state. In the mid-sixties some experimented with counter-institutions. Toward the close of the decade PL steered a course to orthodox Marxism and presumably to the unawakened power of the working class. The unrelieved failure of all these strategies culminated in terrorism, the ego-politics of karma, or, perhaps more charitably, the last act of a lost cause.[15]

Ironically, despite its tactical and strategical failures, the New Left had achieved one success that had eluded all other Lefts: politically and morally it made a difference. The 1913 radicals were powerless to oppose the First World War, the antibolshevik hysteria of 1919, and

102   Solidarity among the Weathermen, whose terrorist extremism seemed the last desperate gesture of the New Left. Diana Oughton and the others died when their "bomb factory" blew up.

the politics of "normalcy" in the 1920's; and the Old Left was prostrate in the face of McCarthyism and the cold-war consensus politics of the 1950's. Although the New Left did not stop the war in Vietnam, it did much to foster sentiment against escalation and to publicize the complicity of industry and the academic community. Indeed, the publication of the Pentagon papers vindicated the New Left's skepticism about the official version of the war. The downfall of Lyndon Johnson, and President Nixon's pledge to withdraw all American troops from Vietnam by the end of 1972, also indicated that the antiwar forces could no longer be ignored. Even though those forces moved from the streets into the halls of Congress, it was the New Left that first set them in motion. There can be no doubt that the New Left, through sustained dissent and resistance, did much to pressure a government into changing its course from escalation to withdrawal in the midst of an inconclusive war. This historically unprecedented achievement was, curiously enough, in the nature of one of the great hopes of the Lyrical Left. "Nothing could be more awkward for a 'democratic' President than to be faced with this cold, startling skepticism of youth, in the prosecution of his war," wrote Randolph Bourne in 1917. Bourne saw in "the non-mobilization of the younger intelligentsia" an "idealism" that could not "be hurt by taunts of cowardice and slacking or kindled by the slogans of capitalist democracy." In the legacy and the lesson the New Left bequeathed to America lay the fulfillment of Bourne's prophecy:

> If the country submissively pours month after month its wealth of life and resources into the work of annihilation . . . bitterness will spread out like a stain over the younger generation. If the enterprise goes on endlessly, the work, so blithely undertaken for the defense of democracy, will have crushed out the only genuinely precious thing in a nation, the hope and ardent idealism of its youth.[16]

The New Left had been no less prescient in anticipating the domestic crises that would convulse America. Many programs enunciated by SDS in 1962 were later articulated by congressmen and senators who criticized excessive military budgets and demanded that the government address itself to social priorities. Thus, by forcing critical issues like racism and poverty into the center of public debate, the New Left made those issues politically safe. Moreover, by making America aware that

185

youth was a growing political force to be reckoned with, it was instrumental in lowering the voting age to eighteen; and by exposing America's worship of technology, it helped make Americans more aware of the peril to the environment. Although much of the theoretical criticism of American society had been articulated by liberals like John Kenneth Galbraith, it was the young radicals who challenged by deeds the subtle methods of bureaucratic control, the ubiquitous manipulation by advertisement, the deadly chambers of corporate life, and the winking hypocrisy of conventional sexual morality. The New Left, together with the hippies and the counter-culture, effectively called into question the whole quality of American life by invoking a "new consciousness."

THE "NEW CONSCIOUSNESS" AND HERBERT MARCUSE

"The young men were born with knives in their brain, a tendency to introversion, self-dissection, anatomizing of motives," wrote Emerson of the 1830's. "The key to the period appeared to be that the mind had become aware of itself. Men grew reflective and intellectual. There was a new consciousness." Almost every generational rebellion trumpets itself as the bright dawn of a "new consciousness."[17] Young radicals of the sixties grew up to discover that consciousness was dead in America and that Americans had lost their freedom without knowing it. This arrogant conviction could be traced through the ideas of some of the intellectual heroes and instant gurus of the era. The New Left's first major inspiration came from C. Wright Mills, a huge, scrappy Texan who built his house with his own hands and commuted to his teaching post at Columbia University on a motorcycle. Mills was the best kind of scholar, a skeptic who never lost passion or vision, a radical without illusions. A late veteran of the Old Left, he learned early in his career that Marx's easy answers to nineteenth-century capitalism collapsed before Weber's harder questions on twentieth-century post-capitalism. From Mills, students learned of the ideological hegemony of ruling elites, the myth of objective empirical research, and the need to formulate a theory of sociology that would confront human relations

186

103   C. Wright Mills, skeptic and scholar who came of political age with the Old Left. Mills is one of the few survivors of the political thirties who gave intellectual direction to the emerging Left of the sixties.

directly and morally. Two other intellectuals also shaped the awakening radical mind of the sixties. Paul Goodman exposed the idiocy of urban government and the absurdity of programmed adolescence while defending his Gestaltist faith in the spontaneous emotions of the young. Eric Fromm gave a pseudoscientific legitimacy to old-fashioned ideas like "love" and "goodness" and started students searching for the self by developing a capacity for "relatedness." European existentialism also had a liberating role. Having read Sartre, American students learned that ultimate freedom is the ability to resist, to say "No." Having read Camus' *The Stranger*—assigned reading for many entering college freshmen—they learned the difference between legal moralism and personal morality.

187

As more and more students sensed the emptiness of everyday existence, their search for meaning led to at least three new avenues of awareness. The tender-minded, having ascended from J. D. Salinger to the supernatural speculations of Hermann Hesse and the cosmic consciousness of Aldous Huxley, began exploring the deeper recesses of mind. The jaded, graduating from *Mad* comics to the entropic world of Joseph Heller and Ken Kesey, decided that to survive the rationalization of an irrational society, one might feign insanity. The radically oriented, taking Mills' advice, translated personal or philosophical problems into social causes. The first option led to hippieland: Haight-Ashbury, Timothy Leary, tripping, and acid; and later, organic foods, fasting, Lao-tzu, Hare Krishna, and Jesus Freaks. The second led to the Pop Left: pornopolitics, Lenny Bruce, the Merry Pranksters, the San Francisco Mime Troupe, yippies, redemptive genitality, and Reichian orgone. The third led to the New Left: praxis and commitment, conflict and struggle as the test of manhood and self, radicalization as conversion, and Fanon's "identity won in action." But what the New Left needed to justify its course of action to all other disaffected youth was a philosophy that explained the causes of alienation and offered a solution to it. Herbert Marcuse provided both.

A scholarly philosopher close to seventy years of age, Marcuse looks like a gentle, deflated Santa Claus and thinks like an angry Prometheus. His role in contemporary American thought is remarkable, for he succeeded in revolutionizing what Americans assumed they had safely domesticated—the ideas of Hegel and Freud. In nineteenth-century America Hegelianism had become a philosophy of celebration (Whitman) or a theology of reconciliation (Josiah Royce). And in the twentieth century Freudianism became a progressive psychology of cooperation and adjustment (Harry Stack Sullivan) or a heroic philosophy of stoicism and tragedy (Phillip Rieff). In addition, both these systems of thought had been discredited when some Americans erroneously identified them with fascist absolutism and irrationalism, and the Old Left, as we saw, had rejected the dialectic as a species of German mysticism.

In reviving Hegelianism, Marcuse restored the respectability of dialectical reasoning, which illuminates the tension between the "is"

104 "Flower children" of the 1960's, some of those who found the answer to alienation in mysticism, hallucination, and rapture, tendencies that seemed naively escapist to the New Left.

and the "ought," between what is given and what is potential, between immediate appearance and ultimate reality. Hegel's concept of the dialectic, Marcuse first pointed out in *Reason and Revolution* (1940), denies predominance to anything by showing that everything changes. Marcuse later revised Freud's central dictum that civilization requires the repression of man's instincts. Basic repression of harmful biological drives may be necessary for survival, Marcuse said, but "surplus repression" is a contrived social phenomenon based upon capitalist domination. Thus he drew a distinction between Freud's "pleasure principle" and the "reality principle." Historically it was necessary to defer immediate gratification and sublimate drives into productive work because of the economic reality of scarcity. With the advent of abundance, however, man's need to repress himself by performing

189

joyless acts of labor is no longer necessary. The contradiction of modern society is that it perpetuates the traditional "performance" ethos instead of transforming work into play and redeeming sexual pleasure, and thereby reunifying man's nature.

The abolition of repression is improbable within the Soviet Union and impossible within the United States. In America, especially, technological rationality has created a status quo that "defies all transcendence," wrote Marcuse in *One Dimensional Man* (1965). Every improvement in the quantity of comfort "militates against qualitative change," for the "people recognize themselves in their commodities; they find their soul in their automobile, hi-fi set, split level home, kitchen equipment." Even the sexual revolution, Marcuse believes, serves only to "desublimate" repressed tensions, to pacify the potentially discontented; *Playboy* magazine supports the existing social order by creating the illusion of fulfillment. American society can absorb all possible opposition, tolerating moral deviance and political dissent but allowing no real resistance. Unable to think dialectically, Americans have become "one-dimensional," conditioned to accept the incomplete state of existence as the highest possible state of being. The "is" has become the "ought," the actual the possible. The "given" can neither be negated nor transformed.

What, then, are the prospects for radical change in America? Marcuse has never been entirely clear on this question. But in *An Essay on Liberation* (1968) his earlier pessimism gives way to a glimmer of optimism. Now it becomes clear that the Marcusean revolution will begin esthetically, arising from the beautiful untouchables, the young, deracinated intelligentsia and dropouts who have cultivated "the sensuousness of long hair, of the body unsoiled by plastic cleanliness." Only they are blessed with the "new sensibility of praxis," an esthetic vision that descends from high culture "in desublimated 'lower,' and destructive forms, where the hatred of the young bursts into laughter and song, mixing the barricades and the dance floor, love play and heroism. And the young also attack the *esprit de sérieux* in the socialist camp: miniskirts against the *apparatchiks*, rock 'n' roll against Soviet Realism." With this mythopoeic image of revolution, with this invocation of eros, song, dance, play, and the beauty of festive youth, we are back with the

Lyrical Left. Curiously, like the rebels of 1913, Marcuse relies less on Marxism than on "Aesthetic Form" as the subversive medium of "the Great Refusal—the protest against that which is." Marcuse speculates, as did the poets of 1913, that man may be endowed with a capacity to make "the primary distinction between the beautiful and ugly, good and bad." With the lyrical radicals he also maintains that the task of overcoming repression "involves the demonstration of the inner connection between pleasure, sensuousness, beauty, truth, art, and freedom," all of which presupposes an "aesthetic ethos" that makes the "imagination" the liberating faculty of man. The "rebellion of the young intelligentsia," advises Marcuse, indicates that the "right and the

105 Herbert Marcuse, scholarly critic of the Protestant ethic and celebrant of sensual liberation, is a leading philosopher of the New Left.

106 and 107   Pop art comments: *(above)* on plastic America—Edward Ruscha's *Standard Station, Amarillo, Texas, 1963*—and *(facing page)* on racist America—Robert Indiana's *Alabama 1965*.

truth of imagination [may] become the demands of political action" and the spark of social change. Finally, just as the Lyrical Left rejected all dualisms between science and fact and art and value, Marcuse insists that "the historical achievement of science and technology has rendered possible the *translation of values into technical tasks.*" Despite his heavy Teutonic prose and Hegelian logic, Marcuse is a poet who shares the Lyrical Left's conviction that political issues can be given esthetic dimensions and that freedom is the realization of beauty as well as justice. Eastman entitled his memoirs "Love and Revolution;" Marcuse may very well entitle his "Eros and Liberation." "The true Left," Raymond Aron has written, "is that which continues faithfully to invoke, not liberty or equality, but fraternity—in other words, love."[18]

But historically the "true Left" has also faithfully invoked class struggle and the triumph of the proletariat. Marcuse departed from this tradition. The proletariat "is no longer qualitatively different from any other class and hence no longer capable of creating a qualitatively

192

JUST AS IN THE ANATOMY OF MAN EVERY NATION ★ MUST HAVE ★ ITS HIND PART

SELMA

ALABAMA

different society," he wrote in 1965. Yet Marcuse also maintained that the student Left could scarcely be a revolutionary force by itself. At most it "can articulate the needs and aspirations of the silent masses" and possibly "induce radical change" as militant students later "take their places as political and social forces in the society." After *"les evenements"* in France in 1968, Marcuse was asked:

> Do you believe in the possibility of revolution in the United States? *Absolutely not.*
> Why not?
> *Because there is no collaboration between the students and the workers, not even on the level on which it occurred in France . . . I cannot imagine . . . a revolution without the working class.*[19]

Oracular, ponderous, erudite, Marcuse hovered like a monad over the mind of the New Left. It was a measure of his integrity and pessimism that he did not go indiscriminately whoring after the young—as did some who spoke in his name. Yet Marcuse's assessment of the political situation in America was nothing more than a restatement of the predicament that confronted the American Left at the turn of the century. Once again we have a young radical intelligentsia without a radical proletariat. Although he recognized the profound cultural cleavage between radical students and the workers, Marcuse still insisted the two must collaborate. In the past the Left at least enjoyed the comfort of an illusion. In the late nineteenth century, socialist intellectuals could look forward to the growth of a revolutionary working class because, in Marxist terms, the proletariat was the absolute antithesis of the bourgeois order. Before the First World War, as we have seen, the question was whether the intellectuals could become a genuine revolutionary class. Today this question has been transmuted.

If radicalism means "going to the root," then the most radical elements in contemporary America are the hippies and their counter-culture. For it was the hippies who questioned the ultimate rationality of industrial society and the ultimate meaning of Christian civilization. Yet it is highly doubtful that these mystical mutants will become a force of the Left, as Marcuse assumes. The counter-culture is not the affirmation of Marxism but its repudiation. The affluent children of technology represent a challenge not only to capitalism but to the basic philosophical and political assumptions of historic Marxism: the validity of material reality, the imperative of organized, collective action, and the inalienable quality of work as the highest source of life's meaning and value. The New Left, presently at a critical juncture in its uncertain career, must thus confront what no other American Left had to face on so vast a scale: a cultural radicalism that is beyond radicalism, a new consciousness that seeks not so much to realize but to obliterate the western idea of consciousness. The Left, which historically signified "negation," has itself been negated. For it must now come to grips with a cultural phenomenon that desires not to transform reality but to transcend it. That the New Left can deal with the paradoxes of alienation better than the Old Left dealt with the contradictions of capitalism remains to be seen.[20]

Notes

[1] Jack Newfield, *A Prophetic Minority* (New York: Signet, 1966), p. 43; Tom Hayden, *Rebellion and Repression* (New York: World Publishers, 1969); the student is quoted in J. Glenn Gray, "Salvation on the Campus: Why Existentialism Is Capturing the Students," *Harper's*, CCXXV (May, 1965), 57.

[2] Dennis Wrong, "The American Left and Cuba," *Commentary*, XXXIII (Feb., 1962), 93–103.

[3] Friedrich Nietzsche, *The Birth of Tragedy and the Genealogy of Morals* (Garden City, N.Y.: Doubleday, 1956), pp. 42–43.

[4] Leslie Fiedler, "The New Mutants," *Partisan Review*, XXXII (Fall, 1965), 509–25; Joe Ferrandino, "Rock Culture and the Development of Social Consciousness," *Radical America*, III (Nov., 1969), 23–48.

[5] "Symposium: Confrontation: The New Left and the Old," (Tom Hayden, Ivanoe Donaldson, Dwight Macdonald, and Richard Rovere), *American Scholar*, XXXVI (Aug., 1967), 567–88.

[6] Jeremy Larner, quoted in "The Young Radicals: A Symposium," *Dissent*, IX (Spring, 1962), 129–63; Clark Kissinger, quoted in Steven Kelman, "The Feud Among the Radicals," *Harper's*, CCXXXII (June, 1966), 67–79; Leslie Fiedler, "Reflections on Writers and Writing in the Thirties," in *The Thirties*, eds. Morton J. Frisch and Martin Diamond (De Kalb: Northern Illinois Univ. Press, 1968), pp. 44–67.

[7] Randolph Bourne, "Youth" and "Medievalism in the Colleges," in *The World of Randolph Bourne*, ed. Lillian Schlissel (New York: Dutton, 1965), pp. 3–15, 64–68; Walter Weyl, *Tired Radicals* (New York: B. W. Huebsch, 1921).

[8] Abbie Hoffman, *Revolution for the Hell of It* (New York: Simon & Schuster, 1970); Jerry Rubin, *Do It! A Revolutionary Manifesto* (New York: Simon & Schuster, 1970); Irving Howe, "New Styles of 'Leftism,'" *Dissent*, XII (Spring, 1965), 295–323.

[9] Newfield, *A Prophetic Minority*, pp. 48–82.

[10] Andrew Kopland, "The New Left: Chicago and After," *New York Review of Books,* IX (Sept. 28, 1967), 3–5.

[11] Bobby Seale, quoted in Theodore Draper, *The Rediscovery of Black Nationalism* (New York: Viking, 1970), p. 108.

[12] Jean-Francois Revel, *Without Marx or Jesus,* trans. Jack Bernard (New York: Doubleday, 1971), pp. 225–26.

[13] Michael Ferber and Staughton Lynd, *The Resistance* (Boston: Beacon Press, 1971); Jerry Rubin, quoted in Robert Nisbet, "Who Killed the Student Revolution?" *Encounter,* XXXIV (Feb., 1970), 10–18; see also James P. O'Brien, "The Development of the New Left," *Annals,* American Academy of Political and Social Science, CCCXCV (May, 1971), 15–25.

[14] Jack Weinberg and Jack Gerson, *The Split in SDS* (New York: International Socialists, 1969), pamphlet; Young *Socialist,* XII (May, 1969); *Spartacist,* no. 13 (Aug.–Sept., 1969); *The Militant,* XXIII (July 4, 1969).

[15] David Horowitz, "Revolutionary Karma vs. Revolutionary Politics," *Ramparts,* IX (Mar., 1971), 27–33.

[16] Bourne, "Below the Battle," in *War and the Intellectuals,* pp. 15–21.

[17] Ralph Waldo Emerson, "Historic Notes of Life and Letters in New England," in *The American Transcendentalists,* ed. Perry Miller (New York: Doubleday, 1957), pp. 5–7.

[18] Aron, *Opium of the Intellectuals,* p. 24.

[19] Herbert Marcuse, quoted in Robert W. Marks, *The Meaning of Marcuse* (New York: Ballantine, 1970), pp. 92, 97; for Marcuse's influence on the New Left, see Mitchell Franklin, "The Irony of the Beautiful Soul of Marcuse," *Telos,* no. 6 (Fall, 1970), 3–35; Paul Piccone and Alex Delfini, "Marcuse's Heideggerian Marxism," *Telos,* no. 6 (Fall, 1970), 36–46; Ronald Aronson, "Dear Herbert," and Paul Breines, "Notes on Marcuse and the Movement," *Radical America,* IV (Apr., 1970), 3–18, 29–32; Paul Breines et al., eds., *Critical Interruptions: New Left Perspectives on Herbert Marcuse* (New York: Herder & Herder, 1970).

[20] On the paradoxes in the Left's approach to the problem of alienation, see John P. Diggins, "Thoreau, Marx, and the 'Riddle' of Alienation."

PHOTO CREDITS

PAGE

4 The Bettmann Archive
5 Dennis Stock/Magnum
6 The Ben and Beatrice Goldstein
Foundation
8 The Granger Collection
11 Top—The Granger Collection.
Bottom—Charles Moore/Black
Star
12 The Granger Collection
13 The Granger Collection
15 Brown Brothers
16 Ted Cowell/Black Star
19 The Granger Collection
20/21 © 1966 Jules Feiffer. Courtesy
Publishers-Hall Syndicate
22 The Library of Congress
24 Top—Culver Pictures. Bottom—
The Bettmann Archive
29 The Granger Collection
32 Top, left—NAACP. Top, right—
Photoworld. Bottom—The Ben
and Beatrice Goldstein
Foundation
33 Mrs. Max Eastman
34 Photoworld
35 The Granger Collection
40 Sovfoto
42 The Library of Congress
43 UPI
45 Museum of the City of New York
47 The Tamiment Institute
49 The New York Public Library
Collection
50 The Granger Collection
53 The Granger Collection
55 The Granger Collection
56 Brown Brothers
57 The Granger Collection
58 The Granger Collection
59 The Library of Congress
62 The Library of Congress
64 The Granger Collection

65 Brown Brothers
74 The Philadelphia Museum of
Art: The Louise and Walter
Arensberg Collection '50–134–59
75 Museum of the City of New York
76 The Royal Museum of Fine Arts,
J. Rump Collection, Copenhagen.
Permission S.P.A.D.E.M. 1973 by
French Reproduction Rights.
77 The Bettmann Archive
81 The Ben and Beatrice Goldstein
Foundation
82 The Granger Collection
83 The National Archives
84/85 The National Archives
86 Museum of the City of New York
87 The National Archives
89 The Ben and Beatrice Goldstein
Foundation
91 Cartoon by Hugo Gellert from
New Masses The Ben and
Beatrice Goldstein Foundation
93 Ben Shahn. The Passion of Sacco
and Vanzetti. (1931–32). From
The Sacco-Vanzetti series of 23
paintings. Tempera on canvas
84½ × 48. Collection Whitney
Museum of American Art. Gift
of Edith and Milton Lowenthal
in memory of Juliana Force.
94 UPI
96 The National Archives
98 Mrs. Max Eastman
100 UPI
103 The Ben and Beatrice Goldstein
Foundation
109 Top—Dorothea Lange, The
Library of Congress. Bottom—
Russell Lee, The Library of
Congress
114 The Museum of Modern Art.
Mrs. Simon Guggenheim Fund

197

119 The Ben and Beatrice Goldstein Foundation
122 UPI
124 The National Archives
125 Wide World
126 The Ben and Beatrice Goldstein Foundation
130/131 On extended loan to the Museum of Modern Art from the artist
132 Culver Pictures
133 UPI
134 From a series of caricatures made at the First American Writers Conference by William Gropper, Phil Wolfe and Russell T. Limbach. NEW MASSES, May 7, 1933
135 The Washington Post
139 The Bettmann Archive
143 Left—IPA News photo, Editorial Photocolor Archives. Right—Doubleday & Co.
146 Left—Photo by Edward Leigh, courtesy Random House. Right—Wide World. Bottom—Photo by Fabian Bachrach, courtesy Harcourt Brace Jovanovich
149 Pictorial Parade
156 UPI
158 Bill Owens/BBM Associates
159 Jeffrey Blankfort/Camera Press, London and Pictorial Parade
162 Burk Uzzle/Magnum
163 Dennis Stock/Magnum
167 Marc Riboud/Magnum
168 Marc Riboud/Magnum
170 Ollie Atkins
171 Harvey Stein
174 Bruno Barbey/Magnum
175 Susan Sontag and Dugald Stermer. THE ART OF REVOLUTION: CASTRO'S CUBA. 1959–70. © 1971 McGraw-Hill Co. By permission.
178 Jeffrey Blankfort/BBM Associates
179 John Filo, *The Valley Daily News* Tarentum, Pa.
180 Wide World
181 Roger Malloch/Magnum
182 Shames/Black Star
184 Harvey Stein
187 Pictorial Parade
189 Susan Ylvisaker/Jeroboam
191 AFP from Pictorial Parade
192 Collection Charles Cowles, New York
193 Collection Walter A. Netsch, Chicago

Index

Aaron, Daniel, 116
Abolitionists, 10
Abraham Lincoln Brigade, 129–30
Adams, Henry, 37, 145
Adams, John, 12
Affluence
and Marxist economics, 140
and middle-class alienation, 157
AFL. *See* American Federation of Labor
Agee, James, 108
Agrarian radicalism. *See* Populism
Alienation, 150
and New Left, 157–62, 195
"America and the New Era," 171
"American exceptionalism," 95, 123,
145
American Federation of Labor (AFL),
45–46
Comintern attitude toward, 99
American history, Marxist interpreta-
tions of, 116, 145–48
American Railway Union, 63
American Union Against Militarism,
101
American Workers Party, 121
Anarchists, 58
and Bolshevik revolution, 90
Russian, 96
in Spain, 130
Antiwar movement
and First World War, 81–84
May Day mobilization of 1971, 180
and New Left, 177, 179, 180
in 1934, 127
See also Vietnam war
Appeal to Reason (Weyland), 13
Aron, Raymond, 3

Art
Old Left on, 119–20
and politics, 75–78
Associationists, 51
Auden, W. H., 135

Babbitt, Irving, 10
Bay of Pigs invasion, 159
Beard, Charles, 84, 145
Beat poets, 157
Bedford-Jones, H., 127
Bell, Daniel, 142, 151
Bellamy, Edward, 52, 53, 63
Berger, Victor, 56, 57, 83
Bergson, Henri, 30, 77
Berkeley Free Speech movement, 156
Berkman, Alexander, 90
Black Americans and Communist
Party of 1930's, 126. *See also*
Black militants and New Left
"Black Belt" doctrine, 126
Black militants and New Left, 173–
74, 176
Black Panther Party, 174, 176
factionalism in, 182
Black-power movement, 173–76
Bolshevik revolution, 19
impact on Lyrical Left, 88–92
and John Reed, 98–99
Boorstin, Daniel J., 145, *146*, 147, 148
Boudin, Louis, 82
"Bourgeois intellectuals," 29. *See also*
Left intellectuals
Bourne, Randolph, 44, 77, 84, 85–86,
87, 88, 165, 185
Brook Farm, 23, 50, 51–52, 69
Brown, Norman O., 161

Bruce, Lenny, 188
Bryan, William Jennings, 41, *43*, 63–64
Bunyan, Paul, 147
Burnham, James, 123, 140–41, 150–51

Calhoun, John C., 10
Calverton, V. F., 110, 111, 120
Cambodia, invasion of, 179–80
Campus protests and Vietnam war, 177, 179–80
Cannon, James P., 123
Capitalism
  and birth of Left, 4
  and Communist Party, 115
  conservative critics of, 10
  and fascism, 114–15
  Marxist critiques of, 138, 140
  and mass democracy, 8–9
  and populism, 43–44
  and working-class values, 108, 110
Carmichael, Stokely, 173
Castro, Fidel, 159, 160, 167, *168*
Caute, David, 9
Christian existentialism, 142–43
Christian socialists, 4
Christianity and Lyrical Left, 78
CIO and Communist Party, 124–25
Civil-rights movement, 10
  and New Left, 9, 155, 168–69
Class conflict, 8, 136–37, 145
Class consciousness, 23, 48–49
CLP. See Communist Labor Party
Cold War
  impact on Old Left, 151–52
  and Kennedy Administration, 159
"Colored Alliance," 41
Columbia University, 73, 84
Comintern, 90–91, 102
  and American communist parties, 94–95
  and John Reed, 99
  and Popular Front policy, 128–29
  and rise of Hitler, 114–15
  and Spanish Civil War, 130
Committee for Cultural Freedom, 135
Committee on Public Information, 85

Communes
  of 1830's and 1840's, 50
  of hippies, 161
  See also Brook Farm
Communism
  in American communes, 50
  and Depression, 112–15
  and individual rebellion, 120–21
  of Old Left, 111–12
Communist, The, 123
Communist International. See Comintern
Communist Labor Party (CLP), 92
Communist Party of the Left Opposition. See Trotskyists
Communist Party of the Right Opposition. See Lovestonites
Communist Party U.S.A. (CPUSA)
  and Black Americans, 126
  and Comintern directives, 94–95
  formation of, 92
  and impact of Russo-German nonagression pact, 135–36
  and labor movement, 123–26
  in 1920's, 95
  in 1930's, 115–16, 123–28
  Popular Front policies of, 128–29
  and Progressive Labor Party, 171
  and rise of Hitler, 114–15
  in "third Period," 123–28
  in underground period, 92
Conservatism
  of American working class, 44–45
  and fear of class war, 8
  Left as opposition to, 15–16
Coolidge era, 19
Corey, Lewis, 116, 137
Counterculture, 160–62
Cowley, Malcolm, 73, 110, *134*
CPUSA. See Communist Party U.S.A.
Crisis of the Middle Class, The (Corey), 137
Cuba, 20
  New Left attitude toward, 167
Cultural rebellion, 23, 25, 75–78
Culture and Crisis, 123

Daily Worker, 10, 123
Daley, Richard, 181
Dana, Harold C., 84
Darrow, Clarence, 67
Debs, Eugene V., *41,* 60, 63–65, *65,* 95, 121, 177
  on Bolshevik revolution, 89–90
  on First World War, 83
DeLeon, Daniel, *29,* 30, 47, 56–57, 65–66, 67, 95, 110, 121
DeLeonists and Bolshevik revolution, 89
Dell, Floyd, 25, 74, 80, 87, 120, 165, 166
Democracy
  attitudes of Left toward, 7–9
  and critiques of Marxism, 140–42
  and dissent, 10
  as threat to capitalism, 8–9
  See also Liberty
Democratic Party
  primaries of 1968, 160
  trade unionist support for, 63
Dennis, Lawrence, 10
Depression, 19
  impact on youth, 126–27
  impact on Left, 107, 111–12, 118, 164
  reaction to, 108, 110
  and Soviet Russia, 114, 115
  union activity during, 123–24
Dewey, John, *34,* 36, 85
  and Moscow trials, 132
Dialectic, critiques of, 104–05, 149–50
Dissent, 151
Dissent tradition of Left, 10, 12
Dodge, Mabel, 74, 75, 77, 78, 97, 98
Dos Passos, John, 64, 67, 92, 110, 115, 125
  on Communist Party policy in Spanish Civil War, 131–32
  on democratic socialism, 122
Draft resisters, 10
Draper, Theodore, 47, 99–100, 125
Dreiser, Theodore, 125
Dreyfus affair, 28

Dual unionism, 124
DuBois, W. E. B., 126
DuBois Clubs of America, 172
Duncan, Isadora, 85, 86
Dupee, F. W., 110
Durkheim, Emile, 4
Dylan, Bob, 172

Eastman, Max, 25, 31, 33, *33,* 34, 36, 68, 73, 75, 78, 87, 100, 110, 119–20, 149, 165–66, 192
  background of, 100–01
  on Big Bill Haywood, 68, 69
  and dialectical materialism, 104–05
  disillusionment of, 100–05
  on Eugene Debs, 64–65
  on First World War, 85
  and IWW, 79
  and Marxism, 101–02
  and *The Masses,* 80
  on Russian Revolution, 88
  in Soviet Union, 102–03
"Economic and Philosophic Manuscripts" (Marx), 150
Economic Research and Action Project, 171
Economics and Marxism, 9–10, 138, 140
Elections
  of 1840, 8
  of 1912, 60
  of 1920, 64
  and Peoples' Party, 41
  and Socialist Party in 1930's, 121–22
Eliot, T. S., 110, 111, 144
Emerson, Ralph Waldo, 50–51, 52, 75, 186
Engels, Friedrich, 49–50, 144
Equality, attitude of Left toward, 7
Espionage Act (1917), 84
Essay on Liberation, An (Marcuse), 190
European Left, 118
  and democracy, 7–9
  and fascism, 115
  political ideals of, 5
Everest, Wesley, 59
Existentialism, 150

201

Fabian socialism, 78
Family, Old Left attitude toward, 25
Fanon, Franz, 174, 188
Farrell, James T., 108
Fascism
    attitude of Left toward, 114–15
    impact on intellectuals, 141–42
    as Old Left issue, 20
Federalist Party, 8
Feminism, 165–66
Feuer, Lewis, 148–49
Fiedler, Leslie, 162, 165
First International, 81
First World War and Lyrical Left,
    7, 19
Fitzgerald, F. Scott, 111
Fitzhugh, George, 10
Five-Year Plans, 112
Folk-rock festivals, 161
Ford, Henry, 112
Ford, James, 123
Foster, William Z., 41, 123
Fourier, Charles, 50, 51, 53
Fourth International, 81
Fraina, Louis, 82, 90, 92, 95
France, May 1968 uprising in, 183
Frank, Waldo, 133, 134
Freedom Riders, 169
Freeman, Joseph, 121
French Revolution, 5, 132
French socialism, 30
Freud, Sigmund, 77, 144, 166, 188, 189
From Bryan to Stalin (Foster), 41
Frontier and American working-class
    conservatism, 44

Galbraith, John Kenneth, 140, 186
George, Henry, 52, 63
Ghent, W. J., 80
Ginsberg, Allen, 172
Gitlow, Benjamin, 92
Gold, Mike, 110, 111, 115, 120
Goldman, Emma, 90, 95, 96, 166
Gomperism, 66
Gompers, Samuel, 45, 46–49, 63
Goodman, Andrew, 155

Goodman, Paul, 187
Great Northern Railroad, 63
Greeley, Horace, 53
Greenwich Village, 74
Guevara, Che, 174

Hacker, Louis, 116, 145
Harbinger, The, 51–52
Hard Times: An Oral History of the
    Great Depression (Terkel), 107
Harrington, Michael, 151, 157, 164
Harrison, William Henry, 8
Hartz, Louis, 145, 146, 147–48
Harvard Socialist Club, 79
Hayden, Tom, 158, 159, 160, 164–65
Haymarket Riot, 57
Haywood, William D. (Big Bill), 60,
    62, 67–68, 69, 95, 100
Hegel, Georg Wilhelm Friedrich, 104,
    188
Hegelianism and Herbert Marcuse,
    188–89
Heller, Joseph, 188
Hemingway, Ernest, 110, 131
Herberg, Will, 122–23, 142, 143, 151
Hero in History, The (Hook), 149–50
Hesse, Hermann, 188
Hicks, Granville, 116, 134, 135–36
Hill, James J., 63
Hill, Joe, 59
Hillquit, Morris, 46, 47, 82, 83, 87,
    89, 95, 121
Hippies, 186, 188
    and communalism, 161
    compared with New Left, 161–62
History of the Russian Revolution
    (Trotsky), 107–08
Hitler, Adolf, 114, 128, 134, 144
Ho Chi Minh, 174
Hoffer, Eric, 141
Hoffman, Abbie, 165
Hofstadter, Richard, 145, 146, 147, 152
Hook, Sidney, 114–15, 116, 148, 149,
    150
Hoover, Herbert, 112, 145
Howe, Irving, 117, 164

202

Howells, William Dean, 52, 53
Huxley, Aldous, 188

Imperialism and First World War, 82
Industrial Workers of the World
  (IWW), 58–60, 67, 69, 79
  and Bolshevik revolution, 89
  and Communist Party, 96
  expulsion from Socialist Party, 60
  repression against, 84–85
Industrialization and birth of Left,
  4, 23, 25
"Instrumentalism," 34
Intellectual class, 23, 25. See also
  Left intellectuals
Intercollegiate Socialist Society, 78
International Socialist Review, The,
  29
Internationalism and Left, 81
IWW. See Industrial Workers of the
  World

James, Henry, 144, 145
James, William, 17, 35, 36, 77, 116,
  147, 150
Jaurès, Jean, 30
Jefferson, Thomas, 7, 129, 145
Jefferson Airplane, 172
Johnson, Lyndon, 160, 185
Johnson Administration, 177

Kapital, Das (Marx), 101, 136
Kazin, Alfred, 145
Kennedy, John F., 158–59
Kennedy, Robert, 160
Kennedy Administration and New
  Left, 158–59, 171
Kesey, Ken, 188
Keynesian economics and Marxism,
  138, 140
Kierkegaard, Soren, 142
King, Martin Luther, 151, 173, 174
Kissinger, Clark, 164, 165
Knights of Labor, 45, 46
Koestler, Arthur, 120
Kronenberger, Louis, 144

Kronstadt uprising, 96
Krupp, Adolph, 138

Labor unions. See American Federation
  of Labor; Industrial Workers of
  the World; Trade unions
Lafargue, Paul, 29
Lamont, Thomas, 112–13
LaMonte, Robert Rives, 31
Lange, Dorothea, 108
Larger Aspects of Socialism, The
  (Walling), 26
Lasch, Christopher, 23
Laslett, John, 63
Lassalle, Ferdinand, 55, 66
"Law and order," 181
Lawson, John Howard, 115–16
League for Industrial Democracy, 121
League of Nations, 128
League of Professional Groups, 123
Left intellectuals
  and Big Bill Haywood, 68
  and Communist Party, 115–16,
    123–24
  conflict with Marxian socialists, 28–31
  criticisms of, 29–30
  and Depression, 110
  deradicalization of, 141
  and fascism, 141–42
  and First World War, 84–86
  historical consciousness of, 34–38
  impact of Stalinism on, 133–34,
    140–42
  and Marxism, 116–17
  and Moscow trials, 131–35
  of 1930's, 110–11
  origins of term, 28
  and populists, 41–42
  and "scientific socialists," 37
  and socialism with culture, 51
  and Trotskyists, 123
  and utopian tradition, 49–54
  and workers, 20–23, 25
  See also Eastman, Max; Lippmann,
    Walter; Lyrical Left; Walling,
    William English

203

"Left-Wing" Communism: An Infantile Disorder (Lenin), 94, 95
"Left-Wing Manifesto" (Fraina), 90
Lenin, Vladimir Ilich, 66, 88, 91, 92, 95, 97, 150, 164
    on class consciousness, 48–49
    death of, 103
    and Kronstadt uprising, 96
    Max Eastman on, 101
Lerner, Max, 137
Lewis, John L., 124
Liberal Center, 15
    and Soviet communism, 113
Liberals
    attitude of New Left toward, 164
    Left as opposition to, 15–16
    Max Eastman on, 37–38
    and Popular Front, 129
    and theory of "social fascism," 128
Liberation, 167
Liberator, The, 102
Liberty, 127
Liberty, attitude of Left toward, 5, 6, 7
Lippmann, Walter, 31, 32, 33, 34, 36, 76, 79, 85, 86, 141
Lipset, Seymour Martin, 137, 141
Literature and Marxism, 143–45
Little, Frank, 84
London, Jack, 39, 78, 83
Long, Huey, 122
Looking Backward (Bellamy), 52
"Love and Revolution" (Eastman), 192
Lovestone, Jay, 122, 132–33
Lovestonites, 122–23
Lukacs, Georg, 120
Lynd, Helen, 108
Lynd, Robert, 108
Lynd, Staughton, 124–25
Lyrical Left
    and appeal to socialism, 78–79
    and Big Bill Haywood, 67–68
    and Bolshevik revolution, 88–92
    characteristics of, 17
    compared with
        New Left, 165–66, 184–85
        Old Left, 117–21

and cultural fragmentation, 23, 25
and First World War, 7, 81–88
and Herbert Marcuse, 190–92
ideology of, 14
issues of, 19
and politics and art, 75–78
and populism, 40–44
publications of, 79–80
style and tone of, 73–75
See also Left intellectuals

McCarthy, Eugene, 160
McCarthyism, 151, 172, 185
McCoy, Horace, 108
Macdonald, Dwight, 110, 164
MacDonald, J. Ramsey, 67–68
MacIver, Robert, 21–22
McKinley, William, 58
Malatesta, Enrico, 58
Mao Tse-tung, 167, 174
Marcuse, Herbert, 105, 147, 191
    influence on New Left, 188–92, 194–95
Marx, Karl, 7, 17, 30, 30, 45, 49, 101, 102, 144, 164, 177, 186
    attitude toward intellectuals, 29
    and Hegelianism, 104
    on ideology, 14
    influence on Eugene V. Debs, 64
    and working class, 39–40
Marx and Lenin: The Science of Revolution (Eastman), 104
Marxism
    and "American exceptionalism," 95
    and American historians, 145–48
    Americanization of, 102
    and black intellectuals, 126
    and Black Panthers, 174
    and counterculture, 194–95
    economic critique of, 138–40
    and fascism, 114–15
    impact on Socialist Party, 54, 56–60, 63
    influence on intellectuals of 1930's, 116–17
    introduction into United States, 54

and Left intellectuals, 28–31, 78,
143–45
and materialistic values, 47–49
and Max Eastman, 101–02
and New Left, 14, 150, 167–68, 172
and Old Left, 14, 17, 116–21
philosophical critiques of, 148–50
political critiques of, 140–42
and populism, 44
and rationalism, 13
sociological critiques of, 136–38
theological critiques of, 142–43
See also Marxists
Marxism is it Science (Eastman), 149
Marxist Quarterly, 116, 148
Marxists, 66
and First World War, 82–83, 86–87
and populists, 41–44
and syndicalists, 59–60
Masses, The, 32, 33, 79–80, 95, 101
compared with *New Masses*, 119–20
May 2nd Movement, 183
Melville, Herman, 144, 145
Mencken, H. L., 37
Middle class
and Depression, 108
and fascism, 115
and Marxist theory of class
conflict, 136–38
and youth counterculture, 166
Millay, Edna St. Vincent, 74
Miller, Henry, 157
Mills, C. Wright, 18, 151, 171, 186,
187, 188
Minorities and New Left, 9, 177
Mississippi Freedom Democratic Party,173
Mississippi Summer Project, 169
Modern Monthly, 148, 166–67
Modern Quarterly, 110
Mosca, Gaetano, 140
Moscow trials, 20, 129, 131–35
Most, Johann, 58
Muste, A. J., 121
"My Father Is a Liar!" 127
"Mystery of John Reed, The" (Draper),
99–100

NAACP. *See* National Association for
the Advancement of Colored
People
Nation, 113
National Association for the
Advancement of Colored People
(NAACP), 31
National Conference for a New
Politics, 173
National Conference for a United
Front Against Fascism, 176
National Student League, 127
Nationalism and First World War,
87–88
Nazi-Soviet pact, 20
impact on Communist Party, 136
Negation and Left, 16–20
New Deal, attitude of Left toward, 138
"New consciousness," 186–92, 194–95
New Frontier, 158
"New Intellectuals, The" (La Monte),
31
New International, 123
New Left, 105
as agency of social change, 176–77
attitudes toward constitutional
liberties, 7
and black militants, 173–74, 176
and C. Wright Mills, 186–87
and civil-rights movement, 168–69
compared with hippies, 161–62
compared with Lyrical Left, 105,
165–66, 184
compared with Old Left, 18–20
and cultural alienation, 160–62
decline of, 176–77, 179–86
and democracy, 9
extremism in, 183–84
factionalism in, 182–83
and Herbert Marcuse, 188–92, 194–
95
hippies as allies of, 162
issues of, 20
and Marxism, 14, 150, 167–68
and middle-class alienation,
157–62

205

New Left *(Cont.)*
and offshoots of Old Left, 172–73
origins of, 155–57
Progressive Labor Party, 171–72
relations with Old Left, 13, 150–
52, 162, 164–68
repression of, 180–82
and SDS, 169, 171
and social change, 5
and social issues, 185–86
and theory, 164–65
and "third world," 148, 159
and Vietnam war, 177, 179, 180,
184–85
New Masses, 110, 136, 166–67
compared with *The Masses*, 119–20
"New middle class," 137–38
New Republic, 113
New Review, The, 31, 33, 79–80
"New working class," 176
Newark riot, 173
Newfield, Jack, 157, 169
Newton, Huey, 174
Niebuhr, Reinhold, 142, *143*, 151
Nietzsche, Friedrich, 31, 77, 161
Nomad, Max, 57–58
Not Guilty, 132
Noyes, John Humphrey, 50

Ochrana, 92
"Ode to Higher Education," 127
Old Left
attitude toward family, 25
and communism, 111–12
compared with Lyrical Left, 117–21
compared with New Left, 18–20,
156–57, 185
components of, 121–23
composition of, 110–11
deradicalization of, 17–18
issues for, 19–20
and Lyrical Left, 105
and Marxism, 17, 116–21
New Left offshoots of, 172–73
and rationalism, 13

relations with New Left, 150–52,
162, 164–68
and Spanish Civil War, 129–31
On Native Grounds (Kazin), 145
One Dimensional Man (Marcuse), 190
Oneal, James, 89
Other America, The (Harrington), 157

Pacifism in 1930's, 127
Padmore, George, 126
Paine, Thomas, 12, *13*, 129
Pareto, Vilfredo, 140
Parrington, Vernon L., 145
Partisan Review, 110, 144, 151
Peace Corps, 159
Peace and Freedom Party, 174
Pentagon papers, 185
Peoples' Party, 41
Phillips, William, 110, 111, 144
Philosophy and critiques of Marxism,
148–50
Pinkerton Agents, 67
PL. *See* Progressive Labor Party
Plekhanov, Georgi, 95
Police and "hard hat" attack on
student demonstrators, 179
Political power
and Marxists, 140–42
and utopian socialists, 52
Politics
of American Left, 15–16
and art, 75–78
and utopian socialists, 52
Poor and New Left, 176–77
Pop Left, 188
Popular Front, 128–29
Populism, 41–44
Populists and Socialist Party, 63
Pornopolitics, 188
"Port Huron Statement," 169, 171
POUM, 130
Pound, Ezra, 10, *24*, 25, 37, 111
Pravda, 10
Preface to Politics, A (Lippmann), 76
Progress and Poverty (George), 52

206

Progressive Labor Party (PL), 171–72
  and SDS, 183
  and Vietnam war, 173
Progressivism and After (Walling), 79
Proletarian art, 68, 143–44
Proletariat. *See* Working class
Protestant ethic
  and counterculture, 161
  and populism, 43
Public Philosophy, The (Lippmann), 141
Pullman strike, 64
Puritan antinomians, 10
Pushkin, Aleksander, 101

Racial oppression, 20
  See also Civil-rights movement
Radek, Karl, 99
Rahv, Phillip, 110, 111, 144
Ramparts, 167
Rationalism and Left, 12–14
Reason and Revolution (Marcuse), 189
Reason, Social Myths and Democracy
  (Hook), 149
Rebels, compared with revolutionaries,
  120–21
Red Guard, 167
Red Scare (1919), 19, 92
Reed, John, 66, 78–79, 80, 89, 92, 98,
  101, 102, 105, 165
  disillusionment with communism,
    96–100
  and First World War, 85–86
  on his family, 25
Reforms, 66
Reich, Wilhelm, 161, 188
"Religion of Patriotism, The"
  (Eastman), 87
Repression
  and First World War, 83–85
  McCarthyism, 151, 172, 185
  of New Left, 180–82
Revolutionary Socialism (Fraina), 92
Revolutionary Youth Movement, 183
Revolutionists, compared with reform-
  ers, 37

Rieff, Phillip, 188
Ripley, George, 50, 51
Roosevelt, Franklin D., 128
Roszak, Theodore, 161
Royce, Josiah, 188
Rubin, Jerry, 165, 180
Russell, Charles E., 84
Russo-German nonaggression pact.
  See Nazi-Soviet pact
Rustin, Bayard, 164
Ruthenberg, Charles, 92

Salinger, J. D., 188
Santayana, George, 3, 35
Sartre, Jean Paul, 150
Savio, Mario, 105
Schactman, Max, 95, 123
Schuster, Max Lincoln, 73
"Scientific socialists," 37. *See also*
  Marxism; Marxists
Scottsboro trials, 126
SDS. *See* Students for a Democratic
  Society
Sedition Act (1918), 84
Segregation and New Left, 156, 157.
  See also Civil-rights movement
Sellars, Roy Wood, 150
Sexual morality of New Left and
  Lyrical Left compared, 166
Simons, A. M., 29, 83
Since Lenin Died (Eastman), 103
Sinclair, Upton, 82, 83, 122, 129
Social change
  attitudes of Left and Right toward,
    3–5
  and Left, 16–17
  and New Left, 176–77
  and utopian communes, 52
Social classes, categorization of Left
  and Right by support of, 21–22
"Social fascism" theory, 128
Social origin and political ideology,
  25
Social problems, attitude of Left
  toward, 16–17

207

Socialism
  attitudes of Left intellectuals
    toward, 31, 78–79
  attitudes of populists toward, 43
  and democracy, 9, 36
  Eugene V. Debs' conversion to, 64
  methods for attaining, 66
  and New Left, 159
  and role of radical intellectuals, 29
  See also Utopian socialists
"Socialism and the Intellectuals"
  (Lafargue), 29
Socialist-communist split, 19
Socialist Labor Party, 121
Socialist Party (SP)
  and AFL, 46–47
  and Big Bill Haywood, 67–68
  and Bolshevik revolution, 90–92
  and Daniel DeLeon, 65–66
  and elections, 121–22
  and Eugene V. Debs, 63–65
  expulsion of foreign-language
    federations of, 90, 91–92
  and First World War, 81–88
  growth and decline of, 60, 63
  Left wing of, 90–91
  and Marxism, 54, 56–60, 63
  in 1930's, 121
  Russian Federation of, 90
  and Third International, 90–91
  and violence, 60
  and Wobblies, 60
Socialist press
  in early 1900's, 60
  U.S. Post Office banning of, 84
Socialist Study Club, Columbia
  University, 73
Socialist Workers Party, 172
Socialists
  and AFL, 46–47
  and gradualism *vs.* extremism, 54,56
  and Moscow trials, 131
  in Old Left, 121
  and social fascism theory, 128
  and use of violence, 57–60
  See also Socialist Party

Sombart, Werner, 140
Sorel, Georges, 67
Soviet Union
  during Depression, 114
  and Ethiopian War, 126
  impact on Old Left, 112–15
  and social fascism theory, 128
  See also Bolshevik revolution
SP. *See* Socialist Party
Spanish Civil War, 20, 129–31
Spargo, John, 30, 82
Spock, Benjamin, 173
Spontaneity, 49, 59–60
Stalin, Joseph, 112, 118
  and Leon Trotsky, 102, 103
  and Moscow trials, 131
  and Nazi-Soviet pact, 135
  See also Stalinism
Stalinism, 20
  and fascism, 118
  and Lovestonites and Trotskyists,
    123
  impact on Old Left, 151
  and Marxism, 140–42
"State, The" (Bourne), 87, 88
State and Revolution (Lenin), 66, 88,
  95
Staunnerberg, Frank, 67
Steffens, Lincoln, 90, 95, 97
Steinbeck, John, 108
Stevenson, Adlai, 159
Stokes, J. G. Phelps, 84
Stranger, The (Camus), 187
Strikes
  and Lyrical Left, 75
  in 1919, 92
  in Paterson, New Jersey, 98
  Pullman, 64
  and SDS, 183
Students and Communist Party, 127
Students for a Democratic Society
  (SDS), 169, 171
  and Black Panther Party, 174, 176
  factionalism in, 183
Suffrage rights, conservative attitudes
  toward, 8

Supreme Court, desegregation decision of, 168–69
Syndicalists, 59–60
expulsion from Socialist Party, 63

Tammany Hall, 79
Tate, Allen, 10
Ten Days That Shook the World (Reed), 89, 99, 100
Theology and critiques of Marxism, 142–43
Theory of the Leisure Class, The (Veblen), 48
Third International See Comintern
"Third period" of international communist movement, 123–28
Thomas, Norman, 121, 128
Thoreau, Henry David, 10, 12, 75, 118
To the Finland Station (Wilson), 149
Tocqueville, Alexis de, 5, 137–38, 147
Towards the Understanding of Karl Marx: A Revolutionary Interpretation (Hook), 148
Townsend, Francis, 122
Trade union consciousness, 49
Trade unions
and Communist Party, 92, 123–26
Daniel DeLeon on, 66
Lenin on, 103
and Socialist Party, 56
and violence, 57–60, 63
See also American Federation of Labor; CIO; Industrial Workers of the World; Strikes
Transcendentalists, 23, 51, 52, 76
Traveler from Altruria, A (Howell), 52
Trotsky, Leon, 81, 92, 95, 97, 100, 101, 105, 133
assassination of, 133
on conditions for seizure of power, 107–08
and Max Eastman, 102, 103
and Moscow trials, 132
on proletarian culture, 144
Trotskyists, 122–23, 133, 140, 164
on characterization of Soviet Union, 135

and Moscow trials, 131–32
and rise of Hitler, 114–15
in Spain, 130
and YSA, 172
True Believer, The (Hoffer), 141
Twain, Mark, 37, 102

UAW. See United Auto Workers
Unions. See Trade unions
United Auto Workers (UAW), 171
United Front, 94
Upward mobility, political effect of, 44–45
USSR. See Soviet Union
Utopian socialists, 23
and industrialization, 4
of late 1900's, 52–54
pre-Civil War, 49–52

Varney, Harold, 89
Veblen, Thorstein, 24, 25, 44, 47, 48, 85
Venture (Eastman), 68
Vietnam war, impact on New Left of, 159–60
See also Antiwar movement
Violence
and Big Bill Haywood, 68
dispute among socialists over, 57–60
and New Left, 183–84
and Wobblies, 60
Voter registration drive, 158

Walling, William English, 31, 32, 33, 34, 36, 79, 83, 85, 86
Waste Land, The (Eliot), 111
Watts riot, 173
Weber, Max, 142, 186
Weinstein, James, 63
Weyl, Walter, 165
Weyland, Julius, 13
Whitman, Walt, 118, 144, 161, 188
Why Is There No Socialism in the United States? (Sombart), 140
"Will to Believe, The" (James), 35

"Will Communists Get Our Girls in College?" 127
Wilson, Edmund, 110, 133, 149
Wilson, Woodrow, 63, 83, 85
Wobblies. *See* Industrial Workers of the World
Wolfe, Bertram D., 122
Workers Age, 123
Working class
  and AFL, 45–49
  and American socialism, 68–69
  conservatism of, 44–45
  and Democratic Party, 63
  during Depression, 108
  and fascism, 141–42
  and Gomperism, 66
  Herbert Marcuse on, 192, 194
  Karl Marx on, 39–40
  Left as ally of, 20–23, 25
  and New Left, 176
  and populists, 41–42

  SDS attitude toward, 171
  and struggle for socialism, 29
  struggles of, 57–60
  Trotskyist position on, 172
  and utopian socialists, 53
  See also Strikes; Trade unions
Works Progress Administration (WPA), 127
WPA. *See* Works Progress Administration

YCL. *See* Young Communist League
Yeats, John Butler, 73
Yippies, 176, 188
Young Communist League (YCL), 127
  and Popular Front, 129
Young Socialist Alliance (YSA), 172–73
YSA. *See* Young Socialist Alliance

Zinoviev, Grigori, 99

B 4
C 5
D 6
E 7
F 8
G 9
H 0
I 1
J